Sowing New Seed

*Directions for
Evangelization Today*

by
Frank DeSiano, CSP

PAULIST PRESS
New York and Mahwah, N.J.

Library of Congress Cataloging-in-Publication Data

DeSiano, Frank P.
    Sowing new seed: directions for evangelization today / by Frank DeSiano.
        p.   cm.
    ISBN 0-8091-3479-9 (paper):
    1. Evangelistic work–United States. 2. Catholic Church–United States–
        Membership. I. Title.
    BX2347.4.D476   1994
    277.3'0829–dc20   94-10551
                                                                             CIP

Published by Paulist Press
997 Macarthur Boulevard
Mahwah, NJ 07430

Printed and bound in the
United States of America

Table of Contents

DEDICATION

To the Paulist Community
who have been my mentors, brothers and
co-evangelizers.
In gratitude.

Introduction

The power of the parable of the sower and the seed has grown clearer in my mind in recent years. I see more vividly the wildness of the sowing, how the seed is being strewn here and there, almost recklessly. I calculate the odds in my mind: how much seed must be scattered before any of it takes hold. The thrill of the final sprouting of some seed, yielding three, six and ten times as much, sweeps over me.

I find it so reasonable that Mark would have begun his listing of parables with this one, for what other parable could context the life of the early church and all Christian life as honestly as this one? I understand why Matthew agrees with Mark and puts this image of the sower and scattered seed at the beginning of his collection of parables.

Who can fail to feel the fury of the sower? One must wonder whether his arms are tossing the seed in excitement, in desperation, or in the levelheaded knowledge that one must not be stingy with the seed if anything substantial will come about. Who can fail to feel the drama of those early followers of Jesus, absorbing the betrayals of disciples who quit, with their eyes turned to the joyous harvest that still would come about?

This parable has grown clearer in my mind because the ministry of evangelization, to which I have had the privilege of devoting a half-dozen years of my life on a full-time basis, has forced its clarity, its plausibility on me. In each of these years, marked by scores of evangelizing projects, I have seen the seed being scattered and sown; I often have felt the tension of wondering whether the seed would yield fruit for the Lord. During these years of ministry, I also had to reflect more systematically on evangelization, to ponder what Catholics mean when they say that word, to produce tools to help facilitate the ministry, and to have a role in the completion of the United States bishops' statement, *Go and Make Disciples: A National Plan and Strategy for Catholic Evangelization in the United States.*

My exposure to both the pastoral and theological sides of the evangelization issue has caused issues to be raised and questions to be puzzled over. The theory, important as it is, can mean something only if it yields more and more evangelizing projects; the projects, on the other hand, raise questions that at least need addressing, if not finished answers.

So I am scattering and sowing new seed with this book, presenting eleven chapters written to stir wider discussion about the import of evangelization for our Catholic lives. This is a book of opinion, quite unashamedly so. If it makes people wonder, question, think and try to connect, it will have done its modest job. Some of the chapters may seem quite theological, although I've tried to write all of them with a practical edge. Other chapters may seem provocative, and this purposely so because I want to provoke the Catholic community—particularly the professionals in our church—to action.

A few of the chapters came about as talks given to various groups. Chapter 4 was adapted from an address I gave to the school principals of the Archdiocese of Newark; chapter 5 comes from a talk given to lay people in the Diocese of Kalamazoo. Other chapters are elaborations of things I've been thinking about (and feeling) for years. In addition, the appendix contains the "Summary Version" of *Go and Make Disciples: A National Plan and Strategy for Catholic Evangelization in the United States.* This has been added thanks to the Paulist National Catholic Evangelization Association which has prepared and published this Summary Version. I also acknowledge the USCC publishing office which has let us reproduce some of the text of the bishops' document. It should help orient a reader to certain references to the national plan made throughout this book.

All of these chapters, however, are modestly presented, even if they are argued with energy. I feel that we need energetic argument in the church about some of these issues; it's a way to show the energy of our church, which is so often hidden out of passivity or a desire for safety.

I need to acknowledge the assistance of Fr. Kenneth Boyack, CSP, Fr. Robert J. O'Donnell, CSP, Sr. Pat Parachini, SNJM and Ms. Kathryn Swartz who read the next-to-last draft of these chapters and gave me directions, suggestions and invaluable help.

There is not a strict unity to the book. To have done that would have meant producing an entire theology and pastoral handbook. Let's face it, I'll have trouble finding readers for *this* kind of work, let alone trying to find fewer readers for something more abstract. The benefit of this loose unity is that each chapter can be read by itself and people interested in the catechetical or liturgical or pastoral aspects can pick and choose. The liability is that some of the points have had to be made in several chapters, although I have tried to limit the repetition.

So I am, with this collection, like a sower and these chapters are new seeds that I am, through the ministry I've been privileged to have had, happy to have in my sack. I'll throw them around and hope that some new directions in the church will, in God's goodness, come about and that at least the church I love will have been served.

1

Evangelization—A New Framework

What difference does evangelization make?

I will argue in this book that evangelization can make a decisive difference in almost all the areas of modern church life. It offers us a new framework, a new perspective from which most of the things we do under the umbrella of church (catechetics, liturgy, ministry, parish and parish school life and even ecumenism) and a lot of the attitude we have toward what we do (our motives and our sense of welcome) can all be dramatically clarified.

This book of essays is presented to explore this framework in certain areas that seem to occupy a lot of the attention and energy of Catholics today. It starts to respond to the challenge: what does evangelization have to say?

Most of the resources of our church today go to catechetics and liturgy, so these topics will make up the larger collection of areas in which we can begin responding to the challenge of evangelization. After all, hard as one tries not to be cynical, it seems unlikely that we Catholics will begin expending our resources on evangelization the way we do on our sanctuaries or our children.

So maybe the idea of evangelization can begin to burrow into these domains, into the way we "do" church, liturgy and religious education, into the way we understand ourselves as a chosen people, as religious communities and as parishes. Even more, maybe evangelization can help retrieve some of these dimensions of our Catholic life from stultification—from the dryness, monotony and self-absorption that characterize so much mainstream Catholic church life.

Not that evangelization means some kind of systematic effort to induce a certain range of feelings or a distinct emotional tonality to church life, even though many people think that's what evangelization is for: making Catholics excited; waking Catholics up; getting Catholics to feel the power of God. These may be dimensions of evangelization, even as they have been dimensions of certain kinds of spirituality all through the history of the church. But they are not what evangelization is, properly speaking.

My basic assumptions about evangelization flow from certain key documents of the church, namely Pope Paul VI's apostolic exhortation called *On Evangelization in the Modern World* and the United States bishops' pastoral message called *Go and Make Disciples: A National Plan and Strategy for Catholic Evangelization in the United States.* I do not want to get into another discussion of the definition of evangelization because enough ink has been (and will yet be) spilled elaborating what is a fairly straightforward notion. In fact, I have spilled ink on that topic already and the interested reader can look up "What is Catholic Evangelization," in *Creating the Evangelizing Parish* (Frank DeSiano, CSP, and Kenneth Boyack, CSP [Paulist Press, 1993]).

The bishops of the United States have staked out a notion of evangelization by saying that "evangelization means bringing the Good News of Jesus into every human situation and seeking to convert individuals and society by the divine power of the Gospel itself. Its essence is the proclamation of salvation in Jesus Christ and the response of a person in faith, both being the work of the Spirit of God." [*Go and Make Disciples, A National Plan and Strategy for Catholic Evangelization in the United States* (USCC, Washington, 1993, p. 2).]

Settling on this sketch of evangelization, let's try to unpack it and see the elements that make up evangelization as a *framework*, a comprehensive vision that can contribute to many dimensions of Catholic life today. I want to elaborate on these elements: good news, human experience, the diversity of the gospel message, God, discipleship, a relational and outward focus, and the eschaton. They seem to be implied in our Catholic understanding of evangelization and they form key parts of the framework, the vision, that evangelization can give us. (For those more pastorally driven, I might suggest a little patience with this chapter since the bulk of the subsequent chapters will treat pastoral concerns.)

Evangelization as Framework

We can consider evangelization as a framework, a complex of ideas and directions that, together, frame a whole range of human, pastoral and theological considerations. As a framework, evangelization can provide a perspective from which certain elements receive emphasis thereby giving a new and sharper focus to the way we think about our faith.

We've had other frameworks. In the 1950s, the framework of law and obligation seemed quite clearly emphasized. God, the supreme lawgiver, sent Jesus who, obliged to pay the price God's justice demanded, died on the cross. This same Jesus started a church with a particularly hierarchical structure that held onto the deposit of faith Jesus left. This hierarchy was responsible for making sure that the faithful believed what Jesus said we had to believe and followed the laws that Jesus left—elaborations of the ten commandments and the laws mandated by the church (fasting, going to mass, supporting the church). Sin was breaking the law; if the law was broken, then one went to the priest-judge, received the penance, paid the penalty, and was forgiven. If one did not get absolved, one suffered the consequences by damnation at the hands of an all-just God.

Clearly, this framework, which itself competed with different frameworks before the Second Vatican Council, has been replaced by others in the past thirty years. The framework of evangelization extends that one which was generated by the great reform of the Catholic Church which occurred in this second half of the twentieth century.

We should acknowledge, first of all, the power of frameworks, paradigms (as they are sometimes called) and perspectives. Consider, for example, what happens when we go on vacation, how our perspective shifts. We use time differently, we attend to sights and sounds that everyday life makes us ignore, and we have a different attitude toward money, spending it far more freely than we usually do. Even a simple trip to the beach accomplishes this kind of shift for us. Or, again, consider what happens when we take on a new job; our perspective shifts as the questions that occupy our minds change. We not only see new issues, we also see ways that these issues create problems and form solutions far beyond the immediate tasks at hand—for instance, how bankers worry about neighborhoods or salespeople worry about the mood of the country.

Evangelization, while not a vacation and certainly not a new job, offers the Catholic something of a similar shift of perspective. Once we begin evangelizing, we see our faith, our parishes and our religious activities in a new light. Comprehensively, challengingly, evangelization changes the way we see things.

What are the elements of the framework that evangelization gives us?

The Good News

However one tries to spin out the meanings of evangelization, they all derive from the basic idea of proclaiming "Good News." In my experience of surveying many Catholics, most of them will give some idea of "good news" or "Bible message" as an element of their popular understanding of evangelization. They will say things such as "spreading God's word," or "proclaiming the gospel," or "bringing good news to others."

What might this actually mean to them? Do they imagine people sitting around reading the Bible, talking about it together? Or people sitting quietly in their rooms going through the book of Deuteronomy chapter by chapter? Does the image of Jimmy Swaggart, reciting his select oft-used Bible verses to an ever excited crowd, enter their minds? Probably not.

When Catholics think of "Good News" they do not even think of what they spend thirty to forty minutes of their lives every Sunday morning doing in the liturgy. Nor do they think of the way those scriptural images, proclaimed and preached over years of successive cycles, have begun to form the basis of their judging and deciding.

Many Catholics still continue to think of the Bible as an arcane book that only special people have the key to interpret; they don't count themselves among those special people. These Catholics assume most Protestants have the key, especially evangelical kinds, because scriptural verses are so easily tossed around; they think probably Jews understand the Torah and prophets; and they assume that bishops and some priests understand the Bible. But not them. The "Good News" is not their business, not when it comes to the scriptures.

Yet the scriptures form the starting point of a Catholic attitude on evangelization, no matter how Catholics feel about their own scriptural insecurity, and this scriptural emphasis is having an impact on Catholics and the way they understand themselves. Given the way the scriptures actually function in Catholic life, what is the evangelizing "payoff"?

Here are some of the ways the scriptures contribute to a Catholic framework of evangelization and, as a result, Catholic life.

a. *The scriptures point to the centrality of Jesus Christ and the Holy Spirit in Catholic life.* There can be no doubt about it, Catholics have grown much clearer in their image of Jesus and their familiarity with the Holy Spirit through the scriptural revolution that has taken place in Catholic life. They may not be able to tell Jeremiah from Hosea, but they feel that all these prophets set the stage for Jesus. They may not be able to get all the five books of the Pentateuch, but they know the Old Testament points to the New Testament. They may not roll around the aisles of their churches, but they know that the Holy Spirit, which Jesus sends because of his resurrection, brings them contact with Christ and the power to live a Christian life.

Of course, the Old Testament writings should be grasped for their own message and not merely as a pointer to Jesus. It would also be far better if Catholics could distinguish between Jeremiah and Hosea. But still it remains clear: the scriptural component of Catholic life today has reinforced the centrality of Jesus and the Holy Spirit.

b. *The scriptures demand active engagement.* Every Catholic, upon hearing the scriptures, must begin answering the question: what does this mean? And, what does this mean for me? As obscure or as boring as some passages might seem, one must think about them when they are heard. This means that our minds, our intellectual faculties, become part of the evangelizing process.

We should sadly acknowledge, however, that millions of people think the scriptures should prevent active engagement of the mind: the scriptural words are heard by these people something like the way a fairy tale is heard by children. They bow their minds in wonder and acceptance. They don't think, or question, further.

However, that method of reading (or, really, not reading) the scriptures should not hide the truth which is that most people, upon hearing the word, will begin to ponder it and become engaged with it sooner or later. Rather than preventing thought, the word of God has had its greatest impact by generating thought, reflection, questions, discussion and action.

c. *The scriptures form community.* This may not seem clear to contemporary individualists who look upon the Bible as a divine equivalent of "Dear Abby" or the horoscope page, as a collection of personal advice or personal ciphers written for confused hearts.

However, the collective and collecting nature of the scriptures are clear when they are used. When read, people discuss them, share about them, probe them and inspire each other because of them. Catholics usually see this happening in the homily on Sunday (or they should see this happening then!). But it actually happens in many other arenas, from parents explaining a Bible section to their children, to people visiting the sick in the hospital and praying for them, to discussion groups about the scriptures which have sprung up all across the Catholic world, to Bible classes given in parishes or schools.

Catholics talk about the Bible and, in doing so, by talking

together, become a greater part of each other. The scriptures form people into a community.

d. *The scriptures force people to look at their personal experience.* As the words are read, talked about, discussed, pondered, people have to put them into an intelligible context. That context can be nothing other than daily life, personal experience and communal experience.

The scriptures are not read in a vacuum. Every reader is an interpreter and the field of interpretation is his or her actual life. The scriptures themselves form only one part of the communicative strand; the other part comes from the events of our lives. When the two strands are woven together, like the genes that Doctors Watson and Crick began unraveling, then communication, interpretation and revelation are possible.

The Bible does not read itself. People read it. People read it in terms of their own histories, their own life stories.

Experience

This brings us to the second element of an evangelizing framework, human experience. Evangelization rests on and speaks to *human experience;* this, in itself, is an enormous contribution to religion and faith life.

The Good News is proclaimed to actual people with actual life stories. It involves them, with their stories, in the greater story of God's working in their lives. In this way, it legitimizes the events of our lives as moments of the divine when God addresses us and involves us in God's life.

Because of this, evangelization must remain open to the full range of human experience since it is from the life stories of people that the good news will be heard and emerge. As a result, evangelization raises serious questions about "religiosity," the poses and filters that religious people often place upon so-called religious experience in order to find it acceptable.

There were good reasons why Jesus hung out with "low-life" types and challenged the religious assumptions of the religious leaders of his time. He was saying that something in their tradi-

tionally-packaged religiosity was keeping them from actually proclaiming God to the people of his day. In historical fact, their
message excluded too many of those who were supposed to hear
it. Their filters kept them distant from the very sins, ambiguity,
brokenness and perversity that they were sent to address.

If Jesus can provoke tax collectors, prostitutes, rebels, fishermen, wealthy women and pious Jews to follow him, it is because
he validated and accepted all their experience as starting points
for the hearing of good news. Needless to say, when our contemporary Catholic filters make it too difficult for us to speak to
people and help the good news emerge from their experiences
(street people, drug addicts, the imprisoned, the marginal, the
divorced, etc.), we too have forgotten that human experience is
a definitive element of good news.

The Diversity of the Gospel

Evangelization, dealing with the actual range of human experience, also contributes an awareness of the great diversity of the
good news of Jesus, the third element in our framework.

This is clearer in the gospels than in most of our contemporary approaches to the gospels. With two millennia of catechesis,
we are all too willing to begin to say what the good news means,
formulated in either a credal or kerygmatic package. From the
point of view of creed, we want to list all the propositions that
the good news entails. From the point of view of kerygma, we
want to outline what people should feel and what steps they
should follow if they are to be truly evangelized.

Yet the gospels show the Good News coming as healing for
some people, as liberation for other people, as community for
others, as mission and vocation for still others. Some people
hear the gospel from their pain while others hear it from their
spiritual hunger. Many hear it from their sin and many more
from their desire for spiritual fullness. Jesus evangelizes Simon
and James by calling them, as fishermen, to follow him; Matthew
he evangelizes by calling him from his life of bilking people as a
tax collector. Mary Magdalene we imagine as a notorious sinner,

but Nicodemus probably did not sin so much. The blind call out for Jesus, but the widow's son couldn't ask for anything.

Who is to say what form the Good News comes in? Who is to formulate the exact process by which someone is evangelized?

Evangelization, rooted in the scriptures and personal experience, insists on a great diversity, a catholicity, of perspectives in God's relationship with the human family. While patterns, credal propositions and general formulas inevitably will arise, the actual working of the kingdom, the finger of God's dealing with us, stands before all of these.

God

The scriptural experience of God comes through the history of God's chosen people and, for Christians, primarily through Jesus Christ. The God Christians accept is the God Jesus reveals, one continuous with the revelation of the Jewish scriptures (particularly the prophets) but one also revealed by the powerful prism of the death and resurrection of Jesus.

God, of course, is revealed as creator, the one who sets all in existence and order. Further, God is revealed as providence, the guiding power behind time and the events of time. God's providence leads to the election of a people to reveal God to the world. From this chosen people teachers, lawgivers and prophets emerge. This God, who is bound by covenant to the chosen people, is also "tested" by this same people: will God stay with them, faithful and constant? Will God's faithfulness be clear to them even as they suffer conquest and exile? Will God, in turn, receive the fidelity of this elected people?

The coming of Jesus stirs these same waters because, as God's chosen, his mission tests the same questions. As the sinless one, will God stay with the chosen one, the Son? Will his death on the cross reveal the faithfulness of God? Jesus comes to bear, in himself, the question of covenant, the question of God's election and fidelity.

So radically does Jesus raise this issue, by his death and resurrection, that he becomes the chosen One for all people, the "first born" of the dead, the one whose experience became exemplary for all human beings. Jesus thereby transforms the image of God from that of a deity beyond our experience, but caring for it, to that of a deity involved in our experience, identified with it. When Jesus is raised, the issue of God's covenant is resolved. Even more, with his resurrection, the idea of God is deepened, because resurrection means that Jesus continues to be with his people through the Holy Spirit he sends upon them.

Christians have seen this deepening of their understanding of God in their doctrine of the Trinity which is a doctrine of the God who not only creates and sustains, but the God who saves by sharing in our nature and the God whose dynamic power gives new power to human experience itself.

Evangelization, which has an encounter with Christ as its center, forces the believer into an experience of the God of Jesus, the God Jesus is, the God Jesus sends as Holy Spirit. Because of this, the arena of God's activity is not some remote celestial realm, nor some past historical event, nor even a single moment's experience. Likewise, the experience of God precludes considering the divine as fate or blind will. Rather, the God of Jesus unfolds in the unfolding of life's experiences which point toward the divine and show the divine presence of the Spirit of Jesus.

Nothing makes this clearer than the thrust of the whole New Testament which shows over a forty year period the transformation of the early followers of Jesus from observant Jews awaiting Israel's redemption to fervent missionaries, roaming over continents, awaiting the redemption of the whole world. What brings about this change is the Christian insight into the God of Jesus, the dynamic God of the Trinity.

Discipleship

If evangelization is an encounter with the God that Jesus reveals, the good news that addresses our actual human experience, then it leads to discipleship. Often people presenting ideas about evangelization assume this, or perhaps just as often, miss this point. Yet the call to be disciples flows inevitably from the proclamation of Good News and the encounter with Christ. For this kind of encounter, this kind of proclamation cannot occur without drawing people together and having them shape each other according to the work of the Holy Spirit in their lives. This drawing together and subsequent shaping is what we call discipleship. People are not called alone; they do not have experience alone; they cannot maintain the good news of Christ alone. Christianity is done together.

One wonders, upon reading so many references to a "personal relationship with Jesus," how this kind of language derives from any kind of reading of the New Testament. Certainly there are personal aspects in the encounter of the God of Jesus; no one would deny that. Certainly, too, many people claim to be followers of Christ without seeming to have much of a personal stake in it. For them, Christianity has become a cultural form and nothing more. Yet nowhere does the New Testament talk about a personal experience of Jesus in the sense of it being internal, "inside-our-souls," and individual. The very notion of "individual" as we modern people use it did not enter the consciousness of ancient peoples. They knew life was a communal reality.

Evangelization demands a context of discipleship, of people gathering together to hear God's word, share experience, celebrate Christ's salvation and commit themselves to the ministry of Jesus. The spread of the gospel is a collective venture. For all that happens inside a person, none of that has reality unless it is verified in one's relationship with others, with a community, with others who also are hearing God's word, walking the Christian path, while shaping and supporting each other.

Relationships

Revelation, experience, the encounter with God and discipleship all have relationship at the core of their meaning. This should not surprise us since human experience is inherently relational. Every human person is a relational creature, tied into others, understanding him- or herself in terms of others, and growing by creating new relational patterns with others.

Evangelization asks that the relational quality at the heart of human and Christian experience be restored to the primacy it deserves. The problem does not merely belong to Christianity; it belongs to most western experience which assumes that things are prior to relationships in our experience. We imagine that relationships spring up later, linking things (and individuals) together.

Yet reality is exactly the opposite. Individuals emerge from the relationships that they have in community. We first belong to each other and then discover who we are, in our uniqueness. The things that we have make a far smaller claim upon us than the community to which we belong, than those people to whom we find ourselves committed.

Evangelization talks about relationships—with God, with others, with community, with the world. It points to the primacy of this relational reality. It brings us into human networks that link with even greater networks, all of them linked into the vast relationship God has with us which we call the kingdom.

Evangelization wants, then, to emphasize the relational quality of our church life: that communities are not church because they inhabit church buildings, but that church buildings exist to make the church community's life possible; that sacraments have meaning because they express relationships and, without those relationships, quickly empty of meaning; that creeds or professions of faith emerge from community relationships and express the tie that we have to those relationships; that the scriptural books are not more important than the scripture's reception by those who are hearing and understanding the words.

Outward Focus

Evangelization, then, because of its relational basis, forces the church to adopt an outward focus in its vision. Because it attends to relationships, to persons, to human experience and because it knows that God wants to address all persons and touch all human experience, it has a restlessness that drives the church beyond itself.

For whom is the Good News? For whom is God's word? What do the sacraments intend to represent? Who should be part of God's kingdom? Who should be excluded from the church, the Christian community, the network of Christian relationships?

These issues create a dilemma which defines the uniqueness of church: that, being formed into community, it must never settle for itself as the whole of community, it must always be reaching beyond itself if it would fulfill its mission.

The very power of Catholicism, of course, results from this restless dynamism, this outer focus. Catholicism characterizes itself by its ability to relate to all cultures. From Asia to Europe to the Americas to Africa, Catholicism has found a vitality precisely as it has encountered new peoples and made a place for them in its vast community. Despite its European heritage, Catholicism knows it can never be a one-culture church any more than it can be a one-nation church.

Evangelization means that the church is culturally aware, attuned to what is happening in cultures and to people because of those cultures. While the Good News never becomes identified with one culture, it certainly has little reality unless it comes through one or another culture. Pope Paul VI dealt with this in *On Evangelization in the Modern World* (no. 22). Rather than fear culture, or running from it, evangelization looks to the ways that Good News can seize and transform a culture.

Evangelization, then, celebrates this tension between the inward and the outward which has existed through all Christian life, that faith looks "to the other" and can grow only by maintaining that outward look. This, in itself, creates both great and subtle influences, making it impossible for Catholicism to become locked in one form (although it has come close to that in its history, to be sure). It must reach beyond itself, its assumptions, its present moment.

In all its church life, Catholicism must then learn not to be trapped by those dynamic elements that pull it inward as community is formed. If liturgy is central, that is because it celebrates what is happening, in daily personal and communal life, beyond liturgy. If catechesis or dogmatic formula make church teaching clear, that's because it has sprung from and has still to speak to actual human beings with actual questions. If patterns of law and custom develop, these have emerged from cultures and communities and must be incarnated yet further in cultures and communities.

Without an outward focus, the church starts babbling and, though the members know it not, starts speaking nonsense.

Eschaton

The final element in the framework of issues that composes evangelization is the eschatological quality of the whole venture. "Eschaton" refers to the "end" both in the sense of "the finish" and in the sense of "the achievement." God's word points us to an "end"—a final and full achievement when God will be revealed in all and humans will attain their fullness personally and communally through the grace of Jesus Christ.

This eschatological quality has been expressed in recent years by the image of the church as a "pilgrim" people, a people on the move, a people seeking God's fullness, a people not seduced by either the present moment or the present era. It creates the "pilgrim imperative" which states that, wherever we are, we need to be moving on!

This brings to Christian life something of a provisional quality, of being in a space for only a limited amount of time. The Absolute, coming to us in Jesus, is not absolutely attained here and now. Rather, a road is opened, a path formed, a journey begun. The journey cannot be fulfilled without God's guidance in the word, sustenance in the sacramental signs of God's presence, and the fellowship of those who journey together.

Is there not, then, an experimental quality to evangelization, to Christian life itself? The achievement of God, when God will be "all in all," when the kingdom will be fully established, has begun and continues through us. But how it courses through history, what cultures it will touch and when, what communities will be formed, what spiritualities it will spawn, what persons it will claim, all stands as open as the possibilities of God in history.

The disciples, then, need not know more than they have to at the point they are. One has traveled first, Jesus the Christ, and the following of him, with a view as far as the road's horizon will permit, is all that the church has.

Moving Onward

These elements that evangelization evokes and emphasizes will yield a view of church somewhat different than one adopted from, say, a liturgical perspective, or a doctrinal one. Yet they spring from the renewal of the church begun early in this century and solidified in the Second Vatican Council. They are responsive both to scripture and to liturgy; they reflect both the reality of tradition and the ultimate goal of God's future.

As the church begins adopting an evangelizing framework, certain questions will emerge and new ways to understand itself and its ministries will inevitably come about. An initial review of some of these questions and ministries from the viewpoint of evangelization is what this book is about. Its tentative and unfinished nature should not obscure the great conversation that we, as believing Catholics, need to undertake if we take evangelization for real. The chapters gathered here try to move that conversation along. Themes that have been identified as part of the framework of evangelization will be elaborated in terms of current church issues.

We're only just starting, and evangelization will bring us to places we've not yet dreamed of.

2

Evilization parish
========

Evangelization and the Parish

The telephone rings and the pastor picks up the receiver. It's the secretary. "Someone's here to see you," she says. "Who is it" he asks, perhaps afraid to sound too anxious. "A couple. I think they want to arrange a baptism." The priest groans a bit inside. "Do I know them?" he asks, obviously not expecting an answer from the secretary.

So the pastor will descend down to the parish parlor, putting aside everything else he was doing and probably putting a smile on his face as well, to see if he knows this couple who want their baby baptized.

Lay people can speak volumes about this scene: how arbitrary it all seems, how they feel grilled by their priests, how one priest says one thing and another says something else, and, in between, they feel hung in the balance of a scale whose measurements they cannot quite decipher. Here they are, bringing their baby to be baptized, and the priest seems so huffy and skittish.

The pastor, on the other hand, feels hung in the balance of a different scale: what he thinks the church expects of him, what other parishes around him do, what has been done in his parish before, and the curious tug between wanting to be kind and wanting to be right. It seemed easier, perhaps, in the old days when most people went to mass on Sunday and being in the state of grace was only a requirement for receiving the sacraments—not that any of that was a requirement for baptizing a baby. Now it's hard to know what practice about mass attendance people actually follow (if any) and Catholics see the sacraments almost as *entitlements*, signs of grace (and forgiveness) from a merciful God. After all, if God is always merciful, why would God refuse to baptize an innocent baby?

16

Maybe, answers the pastor in his heart. And maybe not. Because before he will "do" the baptism, the pastor will feel he has to do a spiritual "cat scan" on the couple asking questions like: do they worship on Sunday; where is their regular parish; were they married in the church; are they registered in the parish; do they use envelopes; are they actively involved?

Couples will generally look too loose to pastors, and pastors will generally look too strict to couples, and between these two views hangs the parish of today.

Broad and Narrow

The New Testament is admittedly unresolved about certain things (the place of grace and merits, say, or the end of the world), but perhaps no more clearly so than over the issue of whether the gates to heaven are narrow or wide. Whole parts of the New Testament seem to be decidedly against elitism. But other parts clearly endorse a kind of elitism.

This issue, of course, lies behind the all-too-typical situation presented above where the clergy appear to some as arbitrarily elitist, while some lay people appear to the clergy as unjustifiably lax. If, indeed, "many are called but few are chosen," is the church calling people or choosing them, or both?

We know the ministry of Jesus himself was quite broad, going precisely to those people that respectable society would have excluded on one ground or another. Even the miracles Jesus does form a kind of inclusiveness that had to have tested the priestly and pharisaic norms of his day. The blind, lame, deaf, and demon-possessed, according to the dominant religious leaders of ancient Israel, were as marginal in the society of Jesus' day as the Roman official's servant, tax collectors and their associates, prostitutes and foreigners.

We see Jesus talking to and staying with Samaritans. We see him at the edges of his homeland, Galilee, working in the Decapolis region, a place primarily populated by Gentiles (that is, the "non-chosen"). We hear him compose parables of inclusion, with seed being wildly sowed, dragnets bringing in all kinds of things from the sea, weeds and wheat growing next to each other, and banquets with guests being rounded up helter-skelter, "the bad as well as the good" as Matthew 22:10 puts it. Indeed, tax collectors and prostitutes will enter the kingdom ahead of the seemingly pure and proper (Matthew 21:31).

At the same time, Jesus peppers these parables of inclusion with other images. After the banquet begins, for example, does not the king go around looking to see how the guests are dressed? And does he not cast into the darkness those guests who are not wearing their wedding garments (Matthew 22:13), even as he calls them "friends"? Doesn't Jesus say to enter through the "narrow gate" (Matthew 7:13)? Is not the path to salvation narrow and difficult? Doesn't Jesus tell his disciples the terms of following him: laying aside their own desires, their own lives, and accepting the cross? Only by losing their lives can they gain them (Mark 8:34-35).

Likewise, St. Paul, whose explicit mission was to gather those defined as outsiders, who pulls together people of highly dubious moral and spiritual fiber (see Ephesians 2:2-3), can go down a long list of sins and conclude that no one committing such offenses can have any part of the reign of God (1 Corinthians 6:9-11). Paul would not be emphasizing this so much if it were not also an ongoing problem in the churches he founded.

So is it for the sick or the well, the sinner or the saint, the broken or the whole that Jesus came? "I have come, not to call the well, but the ill," Jesus explicitly says (Mark 2:17). Are we as comfortable with this policy of Christ or have we accommodated ourselves to dealing only with those we consider "well." If the New Testament is somewhat torn about being both broad and narrow in its mission, our greatest betrayal is to perhaps have resolved that tension in the opposite direction that Jesus favored.

Sunday Morning

We think, perhaps falsely, of parishes as what happens on Sunday morning when parking lots empty and fill, when most of our congregation approaches the altar rail for communion, when people interact, to one degree or another, in what we call liturgy. This is where parish most shows itself; this is where people most identify with parish in their own minds, looking at the sanctuary, greeting some of their neighbors, uttering their individual prayers before, after and during the services.

Who, however, is really coming to our parishes on Sunday? Who are we disposed to see—and to ignore? What happens is that over a year or two we start arriving at some general impressions about our parish and this comes to shape what we are able to see. We recognize, for sure, active parishioners and most of their family members; we can pick out people with whom we have had special contact, maybe at a baptism or wedding; we can pick out, as well, the ones who have stood out—maybe because they were particularly generous at one point or even because they were particularly crusty. So also our lectors, eucharistic ministers, social action committee members, pastoral advisory board members stand out conspicuously, along with a few others.

Who else is there? Probably we will recognize a percentage of families involved in the local parochial school or religious education (actually, in a typical parish we might see only 40 to 70 percent of these people). In some parishes, it might seem as if the parochial school families are more involved; in others the families using the religious education program. So we will pick out some familiar faces from this population.

Next, we'll notice a good supply of "elderly folk," who always seem to be present and who are noticed because they always tend to sit in the same pew or in the same grouping, particularly if they come from a particular seniors' complex or belong to a particular seniors' club. Like mortar, they hold together the crowd that makes up our Sunday congregation.

Like a horse wearing blinders forging ahead on a road made clear because of its restricted vision, our view of parish seems clear to us because of the groupings, associations and familiar patterns that filter our perspective. *We see the people we are conditioned to see.* And we do not see so many others who are also there and, depending on our parishes, might make up a substantial chunk of our Sunday congregations.

Who are these people? There are many people who attend
mass less than weekly. They come every other week, or once a
month, for a variety of reasons, many of them work or life-style
related. Others attend mass weekly, but they are in the city one
weekend and in the country the next. There are, in addition to
families and active parishioners, many young adults, hanging
between adolescence and early marriage, who do not have a
ready-made rung in many of our churches. Some of these may
attend faithfully, but many will be erratic in their worship.

Right behind young adults are teenagers who exist in various
stages of rebellion with their parents and their parents' expectations of them (one of which is their attendance at mass). If our
parishes have youth groups, these will pick up some of these
teenagers and give them an identity; other youths will react
against the very thought of such an identity and sullenly move in
and out of visibility. In most parishes, the majority of teens are
invisible.

Scattered among all these groups will be people who think of
themselves as somewhat "outside the church," because they
haven't been to reconciliation for a while, or because they are
divorced and remarried, or because they are not Catholic, or
because they are just drifting back after an illicit relationship or
after moving to a part of town where the parish is convenient
for them. Also scattered in the congregation will be people who
have no church, who are there out of curiosity or stirring religious questions.

So who makes up our Sunday gathering? Is it the called or the
chosen? Is it the elite, who acknowledge the special grace of
their being children of God and disciples, or the unscrubbed
and broken who are happy that the parish has enough mercy to
let them come, sit, pray, think, and leave in peace? Do we think
our Sunday crowd consists of the called or the chosen?

Parishes might think they are in the business of being the
"narrow gate" when they really need to be the "broad highway"
that serves a wide range of people in a variety of religious transitions. Our very filters about what makes for a "good Catholic"

can subtly blind us to the evangelization challenge that our Sunday congregations put squarely before us.

Evangelization

The framework of evangelization, with its emphasis on extending the Good News of Jesus through bringing people into new and deeper relationships with God and each other by addressing them in their actual experience, challenges the parish on all fronts. It's not that evangelization says that a parish must be both a place where people are called and chosen; even more, it is in the tension between the broader and narrower claims of the gospel that the parish can find new energy in its mission.

Parishes, after all, are communities of people who have been gathered by the Holy Spirit to be followers of Christ; through the celebration of word and sacrament, parishioners grow more deeply into a discipleship of service and true concern for others—including spiritual wholeness as part of the human wholeness we seek for all people.

In essence, then, parishes both result from and cause evangelization. Parishes are evangelizing agents. This means that the dynamics of evangelization, which are both broad and narrow, must become the dynamics of every parish community. In short, the task of the parish is *to draw the broadest circles to include the most people they possibly can and, within that circle, to consistently call people to conversion and renewal.*

Further, in the parish, each dynamic will reinforce the other. For example, only the outward push to serve people and invite them to our parishes will instill the kind of call for change that each believer must feel again and again. Why? Because until we invite others, we hardly can appreciate where our own faith is ultimately leading us.

Consider the following:

—Will not a true outreach to the parents of children in our religious education programs help the program know its apostolic

force? We are doing more than preparing children for the sacraments; we are incorporating them into a believing community.

—Will not an attempt to understand why people leave the
church, to talk with them and reconcile them, not make us keener on the meaning of forgiveness and reconciliation? It will provoke a deep consideration of the alienation that exists in virtually everyone's heart. Inactive Catholics, in their beliefs, do not
differ that much from active Catholics. (The difference is their
practice.)

—Will not some attempt to widely spread information about
our parish help parishioners to feel a pride and place for their
own parish in the broader community? This will lead people to a
greater consciousness about their own membership in the
parish.

—When parishes try to welcome people, will they not become
aware of the importance of welcome and hospitality needed
throughout the whole range of parish life? Evangelization will
teach us what many elements of parish life should be like.

—If parishes can invite and involve people who bring their
children for baptism and first communion, in ways that allow
these people to freely respond, will not that help parishes learn
how to involve people more freely in ministry? Certainly, one
thing our parishes do not do well is involve members in ministry. We beat on people to "volunteer" and contribute, but we
do not make it easy for the average parishioner to actually be
involved.

—If parishes become concerned about how God's word is proclaimed every Sunday and how worship happens, will not this
rub off on how parishioners reflect on that word in their daily
lives and how they pray in their homes? People who hear God's
word clearly begin to desire that word as a daily part of their
lives.

—In fact, as parishes talk more about evangelization, will that
not help Catholics understand themselves in light of a framework of grace, call, conversion and discipleship? This may be
one of the few viable ways we have to get Catholics beyond the

law-and-punishment or the I-was-born-Catholic perspectives that so often dominate the actual way they look at themselves.

This is more than "both/and" because the New Testament found right between its broad call to gather people into Christ and its sharp call for conversion the power for tremendous growth. While we might instinctually moan about how standards in the church are being lowered because we will not hold onto rules and apply them rigidly, the fact is that rules exist only to help clarify one's bond to a community and that the highest standards do not serve us well when they are used to hide, obscure or even distort the face of Christ in our parish communities.

Beyond Parochial-Centrism

Unless parishes recover the "wide net" part of their mission (within which they can more clearly focus the "narrow gate" part of discipleship), they are in danger of losing their very New Testament heritage. We will not be able to read the Sunday cycles too many more decades before recognizing the inconsistency between the astonishing acceptance of Jesus and the rigidity of our own organizational rules.

Fortunately, as we saw above, peoples' hunger for the eucharist and their desire for contact with God bring them to our churches where, amidst people we are programmed to see, they kneel in their own hiddenness. Likewise, for every person in our parish church on Sunday, probably one or two others are also being affected by the work of our parish—spouses of worshippers, or their children, or friends, or even neighbors who all appreciate the church attendance of someone else they know.

Part of the crisis of our parishes comes from the enormous parochial-centrism that grew after the Second Vatican Council. Certainly, before 1965 our parishes were central in the lives of people, but there also flourished an array of organizations and societies that seemed semi-independent of the parish. Because "Father" and "Sister" did everything, lay people felt the church didn't have to be the center of their lay lives.

Since 1965, the impression has grown that real devotion to the parish demands almost constant involvement in the parish. Catholics have to be *ministers* of one type or another, or involved on parish committees, or literally on the parish's property (turf?) in one way or another. At the same time, the growth of a suburban life-style in our church has made it difficult for people to actually feel community in our parishes. Parish means work, with schedules, meetings and trainings. In fact, for parishes to have fun, it even takes work.

Evangelization, however, with its outward emphasis, can help free parishes from the enormous burden of being everything to every Catholic because they have to be at the center of Catholic life. Because evangelization calls parishioners off the parish turf, outward in wider patterns beyond the parish, Catholics can begin to find religious meaning in places other than the parish church—in their homes, for example, or on their jobs. Or with their neighbors. Or in caring for the poor. This may seem threatening to our parish-centered pastoral teams at first, but in the long run it will bring the parish closer to where Jesus was.

The Power of Evangelization

Evangelization will change the way we see our parishes. Once they begin evangelizing, parishes will see evangelization not as some burden but, as the United States bishops' plan for evangelization (*Go and Make Disciples*) says, "the very reason why they exist."

This will come none too soon, because as parishes extend more deeply into the suburbs, and into the suburban mentality, the function of "calling" will grow more pronounced. As we will see in subsequent chapters, suburbanization means that people have options to direct their lives as they want. As a result, whether they are involved in a parish or not, or which parish they go to, will be more and more a product of their choice (or maybe more exactly their whims).

It is typical for people to go "shopping" for parishes today. I have a friend who serves as a greeter in a parish. He reports seeing visitors for one Sunday and not seeing them again for five or six Sundays. Where have these people been? Checking out the other parishes. People in our society will not long endure what seems burdensome and what they have a possibility to escape.

This means that our parishes will be competing more and more as a normal course of their ministry. How they attract and involve more and more people will be a key to their survival. Those are precisely the elements that evangelization demands of parishes today.

3

Evangelization and Catechesis

"If only we taught the children right," most religious professionals hear, all too regularly, from a whole array of lay people and
priests. "If only the children knew the catechism the way we did.
Today, they don't know their faith. That's why so many children
since the council have dropped out of church."

Yes, there seems to be a crisis in catechesis; at least, it seems
easy for people to paint the picture of a crisis. On the one hand,
they have images of large, urban parochial schools carefully
supervised by unwavering nuns; on the other hand, they have
the somewhat less-than-organized catechetical programs that
parishes, through the generous volunteering of lay people, seem
to muster for parish children. Given the emotional weight of
one image and the comparatively less emotional image of the
other, parochial schools, with lots of memorized catechism,
seem to be the only way to win.

People hear about the new *Catechism of the Catholic Church*
and get excited. At last, they say, there will be a simple question-
and-answer no-nonsense approach to religious teaching and
explanation and all this relativism, or sloppiness, or emotional-
ism will be eliminated from Catholic life. (Of course, the new
Catechism of the Catholic Church is not an updated revision of the
old Baltimore Catechism, with memorizable question-and-
answer formulas.)

When priests, sisters and D.R.E.'s hear this kind of talk, they
are caught in their own ambivalence. On the one hand, they do
wish for stronger catechetical programs and a simpler way of
transmitting faith. On the other hand, they know that the world

is vastly different from the world that Catholics dwelt in thirty years ago.

Good Old Catechetics

What, after all, was good about the "good old catechetics"? Well, for one, things were pretty clear on one level. Questions were presented, answers were given and, most importantly, the method used, memorization without deviation, reinforced the idea that all of these questions and answers enjoyed a certainty that few other things in life enjoyed.

Also, the "good old catechetics" made uniformity of thought (and culture) a possible norm. People everywhere (at least in the United States) could respond to the question "Who made you?" with "God made me," and this amplified the sense that Catholics everywhere shared the same faith. Religion tests could be administered by dioceses to all the students; answers could be calculated as "right" or "wrong" with the catechism as a certain arbiter of disputes.

Also, the "catechism format" of catechetics eliminated the problem of teacher methodology and even teacher competence. What one expected of a teacher was simple: get the children to memorize their catechism. Classes opened to the same chapter; the teacher read the question; classes read the same answer and continued to read the same answer until, like some kind of tune, the words stayed in the heads of the children. (Actually, though, we can recognize how this method favored children with good memories and punished children with poorer memories.)

But far more than a catechetical technique, the "good old catechetics" did much more. First of all, it played directly into the sociological objectives of a people at a particular point in history. Throughout most of the 1800s, Catholics were arriving on the shores of the United States without resources, crowding into cities, working in menial jobs, begetting children in historic proportions. Parishes responded to the needs of these people, binding them together with a sense, not only of their Catholicism, but of parish identity and loyalty that has probably been unmatched in church history. The parish, through the sisters and, to a somewhat lesser extent, the priests, formed a large "parenting" society that moved children from lower class and lower-middle class homes into middle and upper-middle class homes in one or two generations.

One didn't accomplish this with candy and whipped cream. It took discipline. As parents had to discipline themselves through faithfulness to thankless, menial jobs, children shared in this same discipline through memorization and standardization of religious practice. The school—and the catechetical method-was an unbroken part of all this.

Secondly, this catechetical technique fit another need, a theological one. It reinforced the idea of faith as "content" and "acceptance of content." It provided the framework in which it was possible for Catholics to see faith as accepting propositions as divinely revealed (and quite clearly revealed, at that) and knowable. Faith did not directly consist in submission to God; before this, it consisted in submission to a church whose authority upheld the doctrinal tenets that people, in faith, accepted.

Faith, then, could be seen as information, as words on a page, as clear propositions, as something objectively definable and attainable. If there were relational qualities (and, to be sure, there were), these were secondary to the informational qualities of Catholic truth. It was a style of life in which dogma preceded experience and the informational approach of our catechisms often substituted for religious articulation and often for religious experience itself.

We may extol the "good old days of catechesis," but in doing so we only delude ourselves. These grand old days produced the millions of unchurched Catholics that populate our land today. Even more, they produced the inarticulate, passive and unevangelizing Catholic that, by and large, populates our parishes on Sunday morning.

The framework of evangelization calls for more than came to be through our classic Catholic school system. It insists that, whatever the method of rearing and training, Good News be dominant. It calls people to dialogue as much as it calls them to listen. It involves them in a community experience which roots their faith experience. It calls them to a renewal that will terminate only with life eternal.

Evangelization, then, forces us to look at catechetics again and ask some basic questions.

What Is Catechetics For?

What is catechetics for? What are we trying to do?

In the "good old days" the purpose of catechetics was to keep people loyal to the church (outside of which salvation was questionable) and regular in their worship. A "good Catholic" went to mass on Sunday, kept out of sin, married in "the church" and passed this pattern onto the next generation. We could succinctly put it: the purpose of the faith was to save one's soul.

These goals should not be put down or mocked. But they do need to be tested.

The Rite of Christian Initiation of Adults has proved enormously helpful today as we try to articulate what faith is all about. Certainly, salvation of souls is paramount. But, today, we do not imagine souls being saved apart from bodies. We would not settle for such a terse formula as "faith is to save our souls." And the idea of "salvation" would be more nuanced than it was. It's not only "sin" and "Satan" we need salvation from; it's the patterns of despair, cynicism, egocentricity and exploitation that wreak destruction on human life now from which we need salvation. Damnation, like salvation, begins in this life.

The Rite of Christian Initiation of Adults, the "normative way" of becoming a Catholic, shows us another picture of what faith is for. Put just as succinctly, it says, faith is for discipleship. If souls get saved, it's because they are disciples' souls; if Satan is vanquished, it's because disciples conquer Satan in Christ; if salvation means anything, it means coming to live, now, a life of discipleship so as to endure forever in Christ, about whom the disciple's life is centered.

In the catechumenal process, these steps occur (chapter 6 deals with these in more detail):

—an initial experience that brings one to seek a deeper faith
life
—a period of seeking, questioning and inquiring
—a decision to undertake a way of life that leads to membership in the church
—the prayer, scriptural study and reflection, the discernment
and decisions, with others in the community, about God's directions in life
—the decision to be initiated into the church
—the intense preparation for this initiation (during Lent)
—initiation into the church through the sacraments of baptism, confirmation and eucharist
—the decision to continue this way of life as a disciple.

Each of these phases happens through interchange with others,
under the grace of the Holy Spirit, in a pattern of growth and
decision. Through this process, people come to understand the
church as the community where God's word is spoken, heard
and lived; where God's love is celebrated in sacred signs; and
where God's kingdom is served through the giving of ourselves
in service.

It is not coincidence that, when Pope Paul VI, outlining basic
ideas of evangelization in his ground-breaking *On Evangelization
in the Modern World*, spelled out a complex sense of evangelization that included, in other language, the same dynamic. In no.
24 of that document, Paul VI, refusing to see evangelization as
only "call and response," says the ultimate transformation of the
world comes about by witness to the gospel and explicit proclamation of the Good News of Jesus. This calls for decision and
conversion and growth in the ways of God. This growth is manifested through sacred signs and incorporation into a community
of believers. This incorporation leads in turn to serving others,
by bringing good news as a believer.

In other words, discipleship entails decision and change,
growth in God's word, sharing faith with other believers, celebrating God's life in sacred signs and serving others in their
human and spiritual needs.

That is what faith is for. And that is what catechetics is for. It is for discipleship. It makes people into disciples of Jesus. Every other good thing that faith seeks comes through being a believing disciple.

Let's explore what this might mean.

The Elements of Discipleship

If the purpose of catechetics is discipleship, then a structure which contains both doctrinal and behavioral elements begins to emerge. Of course, catechesis has a content, but that content is not for its own sake, as if reciting words and phrases constituted anything more than an aspect of Christian formation. This applies as much to recited Bible texts as recited catechetical questions-and-answers.

Discipleship, first of all, calls for *a complete consciousness of God.* The disciple must place God at the center of his or her life; God must dominate the consciousness of the disciple more than any other person or feature in life. Jesus makes this so dramatically clear in his own relationship to the Father, revealed compellingly in the prayer the gospels record from Jesus' direct teaching. "Father, in heaven, let your name be holy. May your kingdom come and your will be done on earth as in heaven." The complete absorption of Jesus in God, his Father, alone explains his actions, from the initial sojourn into the desert to his life's final gestures; to live for God, to do God's will, to commend one's life, even as it ebbs away, into God's hands, shows how total a place God had in the consciousness of Jesus.

Catechetics exists to instill in the follower of Jesus, whether child or adult, this same consciousness of God. Only such a perspective can give access to the moral behavior and communal worship which express Christian life. How are Christians different from everyone else? Why do they do what they do? How do they come to evaluate the deeds they contemplate and the events they observe? Unless God forms the basis of human consciousness, all these considerations can have wildly different answers. While it has become the fashion to argue most moral principles from the perspective of the human good, the thrust of Christian life actually comes not from any abstract principle but from putting God, and the demands of God, before everything else. When Christians place God at the center of their consciousness, then they come to see the world as God sees it and to treat existence as God treats it.

But how does God become the center of human consciousness? Through meditation, perhaps, as ancient traditions reveal. But how many people can become great meditators or contemplators? Through special events in one's spiritual life, perhaps, but how often do these happen or, when they do, how often do we notice them? What can we see from an evangelization perspective?

We see that Christians come to place God before everything else in their consciousness in much the same way we see this happening in the scriptures: *through interaction with the Lord Jesus.* Of course the disciples had a "God consciousness" before they encountered Christ; they would hardly have followed Christ without a very radical sense of God. But Jesus made this consciousness bear upon their lives with an irresistible force. His questions, his sayings, his parables, his arguments, his confrontations with other religious leaders—all this made it impossible for the disciples not to be forced to consider, and consider again, the impact of God in their lives. Jesus forced the disciples to interact with his mind; and he forced them to interact with each other. While Peter may have had a revelation from God about Jesus as Messiah, for the most part the disciples formed each other as they grew together considering the person of Jesus. I suspect even Peter was quite shaped by his co-disciples.

The very same thing happens to us *when we confront the scriptures together.* We interact with the person and mind of Christ; we interact with each other as we try to understand the impact of God in our lives and our world. This happens in homilies; but, probably as importantly, it happens in family conversation after worship, in scripture sharing groups, in moments of great decision when friends go to friends for support, at times of crisis and triumph. We verify each day that the scriptures, rather than being only a book for personal insight and edification, is a book to be read and shared in common. Then its force for shaping behavior and growing in consciousness of God stands out most strikingly.

By dealing with Jesus, we have to deal, at the same time, with the unlimited One and with the limitations of our brothers and sisters in Christ. Yet can there be any other authentication of the reality of God and Jesus in our lives? However prior and important faith is for anything in our Christian lives, faith is verified in the deeds that we do, in the way God's divine commitments come to chisel themselves in the gestures and plans, the intentions and deeds of our lives. Certainly when Paul talks about the emptiness of works, he's referring to our thinking that our fulfillment of laws could bring us salvation. Yet neither Paul, nor any other authentic Christian teacher, believed that how we lived (and died) had nothing to do with our discipleship. Our deeds show our faith!

In this way, another dimension of discipleship gets revealed: *service.* The disciple lives for others. The disciple does not live for himself or herself, nor, for that matter, for his or her certainty or assurance or emotional happiness. As the Lord comes to serve and not be served (Mark 10:45), service, even the giving of our lives, becomes the hallmark of those who follow Jesus (cf. Matthew 10:38). Jesus, in Matthew's gospel, gives the disciples the most paradoxical of all standards of judgment: good deeds done to alleviate the needs of others, even if they were done unknowingly (Matthew 25:31)! It's just the opposite of how we often approach the scriptures, as if they were written primarily to augment our self-consciousness and awareness.

Disciples, in Jesus' view, do not live for themselves, nor do they live in isolation. One does not have a "single" disciple; one has a group, gathered around the master, interacting with him and with each other. That's the way it happens. And if Paul gets the blinding revelation, seemingly out of the blue and seemingly driving him into the desert by himself, the truth is that it, first of all, drives Paul *to* the community of Christians at Damascus and into the hands of Ananias, who, in effect, completed Paul's evangelization. Paul is no religious lone ranger.

The last element of discipleship we will consider here might

well have been the first: *the experience of the Holy Spirit,* of God as
the dynamic force in our lives because of the risen Christ. No
element of discipleship seems more subtle; like wind, the Spirit
hardly seems graspable. Yet through it all—the consciousness,
the decisions, the interaction, the formation, the worship, and
the service—the Spirit gets manifested. For nothing else can
explain the disciple's life unless it is the abiding indwelling of
the Spirit of the risen Christ. No one can experience discipleship
without also experiencing the Spirit of Jesus, attended to in
prayer and obeyed in action, celebrated in worship and submit-
ted to in silence. Catholics, while very rudimentary in their articulation of the Holy Spirit, acknowledge that the Spirit involves
us in the divine life itself—God's love and God's inner union.

A New Curriculum

Our side-trip through some of the implications about the Rite
of Christian Initiation for Adults gives us reason to look at what
we are doing with the curricula we have developed for children
and adolescents. While much of this is infinitely better than the
almost mindless memorization of the old catechism formulas,
and while it has been developed with careful attention to developmental educational theory, the curricula still do not bring
children into discipleship. That is to say, when a child makes
confirmation, he or she probably does not understand Christian
life as discipleship, nor have Catholic children formed the patterns of discipleship which evangelization calls for.

While certain people talk of the "conversion" of children,
even attempting to apply the catechumenal model to preadoles-
cents and adolescents, I wonder whether we can simply impose
an adult model of decision and conversion on those who are, at
least in the preadolescent stage, barely conscious of themselves,
let alone of life-forming decisions they want to make. Even when
religious communities used to accept adolescents into the semi-
nary, they did so with a great deal of provisionality, as if they
were acknowledging that certain decisions only came with maturity. In fact, if we look at what goes on in those forms of

Christianity that delay baptism until a youth is able to "make one's own decision" for Christ (perhaps at the age of twelve or thirteen), we find a lot of evidence of "conversions" happening in early adolescence which are hardly followed up in the years immediately following the "conversion," let alone in the adolescent's whole life.

Children grow into discipleship; they also grow into conversion. As chapter 10 will argue, we probably need to broaden our notion of conversion rather than try to apply a particular model of conversion to every instance. In fact, the bishops national plan and strategy, *Go and Make Disciples,* gives us a rather broad image of conversion: "Conversion is the change of our lives that comes about through the power of the Holy Spirit." It then proceeds to apply this notion to a whole range of changes that the gospel brings about, including the changes that happen when children are raised in the faith.

The upshot of all this means that we can begin incorporating into the curricula of Catholic children some of the elements of discipleship outlined in the previous section. These elements will need to be incorporated in a manner appropriate to the age of the children. But the discursive, provocative and involving methods of Jesus can surely begin to find a place in children's lives quite early. The content, which we must get across to generations of children who are almost illiterate in religious knowledge, can take on meaning as the patterns of discipleship become the patterns of a person's life. Even more, if their parents live as disciples in the home, and act as disciples in the workplace and the neighborhood, the model of child education can only be reinforced by the family's way of life.

In short, we must keep the object of catechesis in mind: a Catholic who lives as a disciple.

Catechetics and Discipleship

Is this too simple? Is it too little to say that the purpose of catechetics is to form disciples? If this is what Jesus did, if this is what the New Testament reveals as the work of the first generation of Christians, then why should it seem too simple or too little?

Of course, discipleship takes on a movement of its own. As disciples talk, they discover; as they discover, they learn; as they learn, traditions of words and images are built up. As disciples consider life, they imagine, they decide and they judge, constructing patterns of behavior. As disciples gather to celebrate, they deepen the symbolic gesture even as the deepest meaning of the symbol gets clarified. As disciples form community, they differentiate themselves through gifts, ministries and roles in life.

Discipleship, it seems to me, can bring us to the full sweep of Christian life and tradition. But that life and tradition, absorbed without an evangelizing dimension, might lead us to overlook our discipleship in Christ.

In the next chapter, we'll explore how some of these ideas might specifically interplay with the parochial school system that is one of the dominant shapers of our catechetical activity. However, the idea of discipleship should not be limited to how it might shed light on one or another aspect of the catechetical ministry. I am arguing that it has to throw light on all the aspects of catechesis.

Evangelization is the process that leads to discipleship; catechetics is the form by which this happens. But only with discipleship has evangelization or catechetics borne any fruit worth speaking about.

4

Catholic Schools, Evangelizing Schools

PART I
THE COCOON

The cocoon didn't work.

The cocoon meaning the Catholic school system that we built over an eighty year period in the United States. It didn't work, or at least didn't work completely. Why do I call it a cocoon? Because one of its chief purposes was to protect us from a surrounding, somewhat hostile Protestant, nativist culture.

I remember reading the text of the sermon that was pronounced at the dedication of a famous church. The church, built in the 1870s, is massive, designed by the same architects that designed the cathedral in Newark, standing like a fortress on the outside, but filled with beautiful, artistic gems on the inside. The speaker of the occasion was some bishop whose name I cannot recall. He was saying to the assembled congregation something like this: isn't it wonderful that you have built this great edifice. What work, what money, what devotion! But, he continued, we know the pressing needs of the time, as the bishops emphasized them in Baltimore, that our children need parochial schools. Should not a parish that has the energy and vision to build a church like this not have first built a school for its children, for the preservation of their faith?

To be sure, there was a debate going on among U.S. Catholics back then: whether it was better to have our children attend public school and have Catholic interests start to influence the public arena, or whether it was necessary to recognize that our public schools masked a bland Protestantism that would, at the least, consistently attack Catholicism and Catholics and cause us to lose a whole generation and more? The sides of this debate are sometimes depicted as the liberal side and the conservative side; actually, the record is more complicated than that.

But pressure was on to build schools as a way to protect our children, our future and our church from what was perceived as a hostile United States. To the extent that it was intended to be a cocoon, it failed.

The Catholic school was a cocoon in more ways than we think, because it not only protected our children from the pervasive ethos of Protestant America—probably the most direct purpose of the parochial school movement in the United States—but also because it reflected and reinforced the cocoon existence of Catholics at that time. We Catholics hung with each other. We were an ethnic church. We were an urban church or we were a small town church. We all knew each other, spoke to each other constantly, felt comfortable with each other, and functioned as a sub-culture within the main United States culture. The only thing we had to prove to America was that we could be good citizens and good Catholics; what we had to prove to ourselves was our perseverance, since we were close to underclass status at that time.

Why did the cocoon fail? Because it worked so well. Between 1880 and 1960 we managed to move children, sociologically speaking, from being lower and lower middle class people to being middle class and now, for the most part, upwardly mobile middle class people. So good was our education, our discipline, our sense of instilling worth and purpose into people, that our Catholic children, within one or two generations, were graduating from our colleges and entering into professional careers. Neither of my parents went to college; my father did not even graduate from high school. Yet none of us children failed to go on to higher education; it was unthinkable.

The cocoon was amazing. It organized so much—our parenting, our educating, our recreation, our social lives, our neighborhood, and even our economic lives. People lived close to each other and felt a bond with each other simply by identifying with their parish or their neighborhood which, in some places, was the same thing. It was a time of seriousness and a time of great order, with a strong hierarchy echoed by the authority of the family and, by all means, the authority of the school, which is to say, the authority of "Sister."

I was a product of that cocoon, graduating from grade school in 1959, at what we now know was the end of that system in its heyday. We didn't know it then, of course, with 1,500 screaming children, crammed fifty apiece into our classrooms, all of them responsive to the same impressive discipline. It had been that way since 1930 and wouldn't it go on forever? Generations of children dressed in their uniforms, tuition free (aside from a few fees), memorizing the same catechism for the same unchanging church, as we endlessly memorized so much for our other sub-jects as well—times-tables, state capitals, parts of the sentence—bound into our identity as Catholics by our identity with the neighborhood itself. Yes, it did seem like it would go on forever. Yet, not fifteen years after my graduation, my grade school was closed.

Before I say what I think explains this, I want to point some-thing out. *Parochial schools back then had an inherent relationship with the parish.* It wasn't only that the school's finances were con-nected to the parish's, that the structure of the school's organiza-tion was Pastor-Principal-Assistant Principal. It was that you couldn't be in the school without at the same time being in the church, in the parish, in the sanctuary. Whether it was Sister checking on Monday to see who went to mass on Sunday, or First Friday mass, or Stations of the Cross during Lent, or the awesome and awful task of hearing the confessions of a thou-sand children in half a morning; in countless ways, the school children were part of the sanctuary.

What did we produce with this? Were we evangelizing chil-dren? How so? Was the success rate much higher than the suc-cess rate we experience now?

People will instinctually want to answer that there has obvi-ously been a tremendous fall-off of the effectiveness of the church and religious education since those heady days of the 1950s. It may not be so easy to be so sure. Most of the grade school classmates I had ceased being active Catholics in the sense of frequent worshippers, many of them even before they got out of eighth grade. The drop-off rate for mass attendance after grade school was notorious. Even when we look at statistics from back then, we can see that, if 80% went to mass on Sunday, only a little more than 40% went to communion. Did we take communion more seriously back then, or was it not also the case that a lot of people worshipped out of habit, convention and obligation, with only a minimum religious investment in what we were all about? If there's any merit in my line of thinking, then we may be a little ahead at this point, at least in some places.

What do I think happened? It wasn't only the liberating influence of Vatican II, or the debilitating consequential breakup of a whole system of Catholic life and education. It was also this: *the cocoon didn't work; we educated ourselves right out of our cities and right into the suburbs.* We have become, in this culture, a suburban church without hardly realizing it, all the while maintaining dated, urban images of what church and school are about.

Today we see no churches opening in cities; we see some churches opening in suburbs, however. We see few schools opening in suburbs, but we see quite a few schools closing in the cities. In our Catholic schools, particularly in the city, children of various Christian and non-Christian backgrounds get a good, solid education and a good orientation to values. But because the population is not homogeneous, we feel a lot of tension between espousing an explicitly Catholic orientation in a population that is quite diverse. Some schools in Washington, DC, have student populations that are only 20% Catholic. It's hard, in this situation, to know what a Catholic school is, at least in terms of the way it was in the golden days.

Where are the Catholics? In the *suburbs,* that's where we are. Looking like suburbanites, buying like suburbanites, working like suburbanites, choosing like suburbanites, marrying and divorcing like suburbanites, espousing general suburbanite values. I am not an expert sociologist and I do not want to seem to define a whole layer of society with a few glib terms; in fact I know that the suburbs contain very diverse types of peoples. But

I will argue this: the nature of the suburbs is to pick and choose, to design life by convenience, to have people lay options out before us so we can see what our preferences are, to be part of a class whose allegiance is more to its life-style than to the elements that make that life-style possible.

That is the kind of people we have become. Catholics have so bettered themselves through their school system that they are now part of the suburban church with two clear consequences: a) our urban parishes are leftovers, unable to be for Catholics there what they were for my generation; and b) people's whole relationship to parish and church is now defined by their life-style, whereas it used to be the other way around: the life-style was once defined by the parish and the church.

So what? What has any of this to do with evangelization? If evangelization is *the process of making disciples, and if disciples are known because they assemble together in worshipping communities and support each other's faith, and if eucharist is an essential part of this,* then what we have been saying has a lot to say about evangelization and the task that lies in front of us in terms of Catholic schools today. Here are some considerations:

1) *In terms of the school's relationship to the parish:*
—How is, or how can, the school be related to sanctuary once again? That is to say, how can people see the school as a dynamic dimension of a community of disciples?
—What is the consequence of making schools financially separate from the parish? Does this also make them emotionally separate?
—How does parish welcome school? How does school welcome the parish? *Do* they even welcome each other?

2) *In terms of the breakdown of our ethnic, urban base:*
—Now that we don't have our ethnicity or social class to cohere us, what will cohere us as Catholics? Will faith become for us an experience of conversion, of choosing to be part of Christ's community? How are people called to conversion in our parishes? In our schools?

—Suburban existence demands that we call people and ask them to choose and *commit*. Otherwise, people just pick and choose, they float, they don't belong and they don't have to belong.

3) *In terms of the ways religion is taught in schools:*
—What does religious education mean for us? Is the education model which our schools force upon us the best way to talk about bringing people into discipleship? Is it learning? Is it class? Or is it active participation in a community? How do we bring children into an experience of active participation with others in their faith? Do we look for a catechism *redivivus* with the assumption that, if we are all saying the same thing because we've all memorized the same thing, then we are all evangelized?

4) *In terms of the impact of evangelization:*
—Do we even think our schools are in the business of evangelization? Or have they mostly become good alternatives to more expensive private schools, even for the Catholics that attend them? Does not the idea of an evangelizing school presume that our teachers are evangelized? Does it not also have to invite the family into evangelization?

The dramatic changes we have experienced in the Catholic Church in the last thirty years, with consequent dramatic changes in our Catholic schools, have done at least one thing: they have torn off the cultural forms which created a lot of assumptions about Catholic schools and have left us staring at them with fewer assumptions. We know a good percentage of our children and families in Catholic schools do not worship regularly, if that is an acceptable standard of being a disciple. We know our schools cannot serve some of the people who need them most and will continue to become accessible only for those with more and more money. We know that our teachers pick up our own ambivalence about the exact purpose of Catholic schools and we are at a loss to know how to resolve that ambivalence.

Evangelization will force upon us, principals and pastors, religious and lay teachers, parents and students, a conversation about what our schools are fundamentally about. As we have this conversation, evangelization will begin to happen, first to us, as we are driven anew by considerations about the good news of Jesus, and through us to a new generation of Catholics.

PART II
THE PLAN

Although it does not explicitly delve into the issue, we need to explore how the United States bishops' national plan and strategy on evangelization, *Go and Make Disciples: A National Plan and Strategy for Catholic Evangelization in the United States* (USCC, Washington, 1993) might influence Catholic schools.

This document is not long and it is written for the non-specialist; this means that our staffs should be able to read it, discuss it and act upon it. Also, if we are willing, can our school parents. The bishops did this deliberately. Everyone wants to think of evangelization as some specialized kind of activity that only experts can engage in. In the almost twenty years since Pope Paul VI issued *On Evangelization in the Modern World*, the first great church document explicitly devoted to evangelization, this movement has had only a sputtering kind of success in Catholic circles. While more Catholics realize that something like evangelization is essential, they are scared of the term and even more scared of what the term will mean for them.

The reason? Because Catholics do not by and large think of themselves as disciples, as people who have been called by Christ and equipped by him to continue doing his ministry in the world today. They have been well trained to be the sheep that ably follow their pastors, as long as the pastors don't ask too much of them and as long as the pastors, professionals, religious and educators take the heat. That's why they put money in the collection and that's why they pay tuition: "You do it, Father, you do it Sister, you do it, DRE."

But in fact evangelization has everything to do with where lay people actually are—in their homes and workplaces. Evangelization can be seen as the initial steps that lead people to discipleship as well as continued growth in discipleship. But if we talk to people who come to the Rite of Christian Initiation of Adults or people who return to the church, they will all tell you the same thing—they were moved to actually come to the church by friends and neighbors. By lay people. By non-specialists. It's not as if faith only happens on church property. Rather, with Christianity, what happens in the church only solidifies what has been happening all along in someone's daily life, through contact with ordinary Catholics.

In light of this, it obviously would make little sense to write a document which was not addressed to the ordinary Catholic. To create a welcoming, accepting, compassionate, involving and sanctifying community, which reflects the face of Jesus today, has to be a key for any evangelizing strategy. And this is everyone's responsibility. A further implication of this: if evangelization wants to touch the lives of ordinary Catholics, it has to have a central place in the thinking of Catholic schools where, in part, tomorrow's ordinary Catholics are being formed. So the plan, which is written for everyone to read, was also written so particular groups of Catholics, schools and institutions, could also be influenced by it.

The plan has three goals which spring from a distinctly Catholic understanding of evangelization. We do not look on evangelization only as inviting people to a personal relationship with Jesus. In addition, we invite them to a life of discipleship, in community with other disciples, being sustained by the sacraments of the Lord's presence and the goals of mission and service which are the signs of a person maturing in his or her discipleship. In fact, as we understand it, there is no relationship with Jesus that is not being verified by a life of discipleship, of involvement in church and in service of others. Religion is not ultimately for our own selves, or to make our own selves feel better about ourselves. Religion, faith, grace are for the world and, therefore, for the other.

So what do we want to accomplish in evangelization? How do

we bring about the transformation of individuals and society by the gospel message? The national plan gives us broad directions in the three goals which tie the plan together. First, the renewal of Catholics in their own faith so that they have the enthusiasm to share their faith; second, the effective inviting of people to experience Jesus in the Catholic Church; and third, the greater impact of our Catholic faith and values on our daily life and our world.

What the bishops didn't do was spell out in detail how these three goals work themselves out in actual life. They didn't because they couldn't. So varied are the situations, so multiple the experiences, so different the parishes of the United States that there was no alternative but to draw up a plan that worked by forcing each group, each entity, each institution to incarnate those goals in their own way. That is why the plan has a distinct structure: the goals are followed by general objectives; the objectives are followed by a list of possible strategies. All this is done to have groups and institutions develop their own specific objectives and their own strategies according to their local circumstances.

It's not my job to tell school personnel how to evangelize in schools; it's my job to say what evangelization means for us as Catholics in parishes and schools. How each school operates, the kind of children it serves, its relationships to parents and parish differs so widely that were I to say specific things, people would have no choice but to specifically reject them as "not fitting my situation." We will know what fits our particular situations when we, our teachers and our parents, and perhaps even some of our students, sit around with the plan, develop our own objectives as they make sense in terms of the three broad evangelizing goals.

Goal One

Let me open up some of the ways this conversation might go, however. Let's look at goal one again: to create enthusiasm for the faith in Catholics such that they want to share it. What kind of enthusiasm? Something like the enthusiasm of the convert because evangelization is all about conversion. But how can we be talking about conversion which focuses on individual adults who make a decision when we are educating children? Exactly. We Catholics do not have a consistently conversionist perspective. (We'll be talking about conversion in chapter 10.)

In fact, if we look at our general Catholic life and history, we have evangelized more people through culture than through conversion—through the structures of family, child-rearing, education, worldview, collective identity, art and other cultural forms. Schools are cultural entities; while some people talk about the conversion of children, I think that this idea gets fuzzier the more you look at it.

Yet conversion does happen through our culture; Fr. Kenneth Boyack, CSP, and I have a small book which tries to help Catholics, through a simple journaling experience, begin to know they have a story of faith and a story they can share. This would be a rewarding exercise for our teachers to go through, particularly our religion teachers. Our book is called *Discovering My Experience of God: Awareness and Witness* (Paulist, Mahwah, 1993). When we think about it, in our parochial schools we are actually doing the same thing as the Rite of Christian Initiation of Adults, but in a different order. The result is the same: at the end of all the sacraments of initiation, we should have an evangelized person. We are actually involved in the work of conversion.

Or are we? Do we need to rethink catechetics from the point of view of the catechumenate and the goal of creating disciples? The more we work with an education model of religious education, the more we will have children looking on religion as work, as class, as something they get graded for and as something they will graduate out of. Isn't it true that confirmation is exactly that in the mind of our children—graduation? They don't have to go any more.

What about introducing more sharing and faith sharing in our religious education experiences? What about having more of those experiences outside the classroom? What about letting our children "play with" the scriptures in their own lives, what people refer to as "breaking open the word"? What about employing more ritual in the classroom? Even more, what about marking the passing of grades with some of the rituals that the Rite of Initiation gives us? If we are asking for commitment from our children as they mature, confirmation, which usually ends the initiating sequence of sacraments, may finally come to look more like a natural sacrament of commitment, of sealing.

Goal Two

The second goal talks about effectively inviting people to experience Jesus. This has two immediate implications: tying our schools into our parishes much more directly than they are and calling our parents to conversion along with their children. How can we be evangelizing the children when the parents are not being evangelized? It is no secret that many of the parents of our school children do not worship, scarcely pray, and have a hard time reflecting the values we think we are instilling in the children.

Even if our parents are non-Catholic, we have to call them to conversion. We need to involve them in the evangelization experiences of their children. If they have a faith community, we must call them to worship in that faith community. If they say they are Baptist or Lutheran, we will welcome their children but we ask that they practice their faith, or else they are counteracting our efforts and their own substantial investment in the child.

How do we call parents to conversion during the school year? What if religious experiences of families were a part of the Catholic school experience? What if several Saturdays were spent bringing families together in faith? Of course, this should not fall exclusively on overworked school personnel, but school personnel might be points for organizing these experiences and the other resources of the parishes could come into play.

Goal Three

The third goal talks about the impact of faith in daily life. This translates immediately into the kind of family life lived among our parishioners. We know how skimpy this is. Yet if our children were in homes that reinforced their faith and if faith were dominant in the home, how much more readily would others come to know of the Catholic faith? How much more obvious would its strengths, values and practices be.

Parents need to develop their own spirituality, but our schools can help them. We can be guiding families in prayer, home rituals, service and sharing that should characterize our Catholic families. Can our home-and-school committees, which spend so much time on social activities or raising funds, not spend a little time on stimulating faith in the home?

Likewise, can our school children not be involved in service, in caring for others, on their own level, all the way through their religious experiences, rendering service to the wider society in which Catholics now have such a prominent place? I'm not talking about returning to the famous pagan babies, but about stimulating the discipling mentality in our students and families by helping them experience service as a regular part of their development rather than an extra hurdle to go through before confirmation. This might pay off in their future attitudes toward faith in their workplace.

Christian Community

In the end, it might be time for a radical new attitude about our schools. It might be time to begin treating them as communities of faith, centers of the lives of so many Catholic families and other families who are now "in the Catholic sphere" whether they see that explicitly or not. Catholic schools live faith; Catholic schools spread faith; Catholic schools serve as centers of faith for millions of people.

So why not bring the sanctuary into the school? Why not make the school its own faith community, its own parish? Instead of trying to get children to trudge over to the parish church for worship, why not make worship part of what a school does?

The image here is of the mission chapel that many rural

parishes administer because of the great geographical distances that rural life imposes. Cannot our schools be mission chapels? Their particular focus would be the families of the children who attend there, but they can also be a center for all parish families and for youth ministry. Let families have their own liturgy in which they celebrate and take leadership. Involve the children in their own mass. Let the school celebrate the life that it lives throughout the week. One of the priests can serve as chaplain as part of his work profile in the parish.

Of course, this would happen only for eight months and it perhaps should not happen every Sunday. But this might bring to the Catholic school exactly what has been missing for almost twenty years. God knows, our suburban parishes are overcrowded as it is and developing a mission chapel would alleviate some of that even as it served as a clearer way to call Catholic families, school families and all families to conversion and growth in Christ.

Schools can be evangelizing communities and evangelization may be one idea that can help the Catholic school today recover its legacy, albeit in a different time and different culture. The goals our bishops have proposed for us can shift the emphases of our schools because they shift the emphases in our own heads about what we are all about.

Evangelization can begin as a process of principals sitting with their teachers, parents, parish leaders and students and looking at how these three goals are already working in our schools and how they can challenge them further. Jesus wanted his disciples to be like wise stewards who could bring from their pantries both the old and the new. What Catholic schools and Catholic education are all about can achieve its age-old purpose of helping to make disciples by facing the challenge of evangelization and becoming evangelizing schools and evangelizing ministries.

5

Evangelization and Welcoming

In one of the most dramatic passages of the New Testament, Jesus makes quite a big deal of welcoming. Simon invited Jesus to his house, but it must have been out of social obligation; when Jesus got there, Simon hardly paid him any attention and, the passage seems to hint, not many others paid Jesus much attention either. (See Luke 7:37–50.)

Not many paid attention except one of the local ladies, perhaps a lady of the street, perhaps just a woman with a complex and hard-to-understand past. She came up to Jesus, walking through the crowd of religiously righteous people, and knelt behind him. Simon then looked at Jesus, curious what this prophet from Galilee would do. "If he were a prophet," Simon thinks to himself, "he'd surely know what kind of woman was touching him."

After Jesus gives Simon a lesson about compassion, forgiveness and love, he decides to give him another lesson, about welcoming. It's almost as if Jesus is saying that welcoming people is wrapped up with compassion and love. He points out to Simon that, when he came, no bowl was provided so Jesus could wash his feet, but this sinful woman has not stopped washing the feet of Jesus with her tears. Nor did Simon give him a simple embrace of welcome, but this sinner has not stopped embracing his feet. And Simon did not put perfumed ointment on his head, but this woman, whose sight makes Simon cringe, has anointed the feet of Jesus with precious perfume.

Put bluntly, Simon did not know how to welcome whereas the sinner could not stop welcoming.

We know how we feel when we've been invited to a party at

50

which we uncomfortably discover we know no one. We feel awkward, thinking everyone is watching us. We try to smile, but people do not seem to be smiling back so quickly. We sense they are not even making simple eye contact. We wander up to people and try to begin a conversation, all the while fearing that we'll be judged a bore or say something that inadvertently will seem wrong. By the time the party ends, we're exhausted. We've worked so hard trying to orient ourselves, we have no energy left.

What a difference a process of welcoming can make. Welcoming is a certain kind of orientation that says a person belongs, has a place, and even has a special place, with others. It gives people who feel unconnected a starting connection. Even though guests still feel strange as they try to understand new people in new surroundings, a warm welcome, because of its special emphasis, compensates for that awkwardness. The group is saying: "We know you are new, so try to relax. We'll make special efforts so you can feel at home."

While welcome obviously doesn't always mean compassion and forgiveness, it's easy to see that, without welcome, compassion and forgiveness have no foundation. Certainly, compassion and forgiveness demand connections, a sense of people at one with each other. By definition, compassion means that one person can sense the feelings of another—a unity of emotion. Forgiveness means that two or more people overcome barriers and make peace with each other—a return to unity. But if welcome has never been given, if people do not even have the chance to feel at one, with a group, how can compassion or forgiveness ever have a start?

Maybe that's why Simon, inhospitable as he was, would never think that such a sinful woman could be forgiven. Forgiveness for someone so alien to him could not even cross his mind. And maybe that's why Simon himself did not experience God's forgiveness very much. "To the one who loves little, little has been forgiven," says Jesus. People with small hearts haven't the ability to understand how God's forgiveness works. People without the simple ability to include another person indeed have very small hearts.

Welcome in Our Parishes

With so few places where modern people informally congregate, parishes enjoy a special place in today's life. They at least establish neutral territory in that everyone can go there; it's a public, accessible space. Yet parishes represent more than neutral territory because there people concentrate on the central truths of their lives and, because of this, feel a great bonding with others who have discovered the same fundamental truths of their lives. Our language in church, calling each other "beloved" and "brothers and sisters," speaks eloquently about the way we intend to see ourselves when we come together in community at the parish.

This very same language, however, can seem like sheer hype when we use it to measure the generally impersonal and anonymous experiences that many have of parishes today. Catholic parishioners typically enter a quasi-dark, silent building and automatically drift to their familiar pew. They stare straight ahead. Perhaps one family member may make a gesture or some remark to another. If acquaintances enter the church, parishioners may wave a hand or nod a head. To most everyone else, they are stone dead.

To many parishioners even the mass seems an obligation, with people coming as late as they can and leaving as early as local custom will allow. In some parishes, I've seen many people receive their host and exit immediately out the side door, totally oblivious to what this is saying to the rest of the community. "We've had enough of you. We cannot wait to get out." Responses during the eucharist go unmade, songs go unsung, the sign of peace is given begrudgingly.

Connection? Bondedness? A sense of others? Compassion? If Catholics rarely feel these things at their parish, maybe the absence of a sense of welcome has something to do with this.

We will look at three areas in which most parishes can

increase their welcoming activity. This will more greatly open to them the direction which modern liturgy and spirituality are setting. It will also open up some of the basic dynamics of evangelization which seeks to bring Good News to people in the actual situations of their lives.

Welcoming New Parishioners

Given the importance parish has for the faith of Catholics, particularly in view of their historical importance in the United States, the process by which Catholics join parishes today can only be described as scandalous. Potential new parishioners approach the priest after mass, as he's passing little *bon-mots* to the parishioners he already knows as they leave. "Father, how can we join the parish?" they ask. "Call the secretary on Monday," he calls back. Or, "Jot down your name and phone number on this bulletin and I'll see you get listed."

"Getting listed" is just about what happens too. The secretary puts into the computer, or onto index cards, the name of the family; she assigns an envelope number, and puts them on the mailing list. In addition, many parishes will try to get information from the family through the use of something like a standard census form which asks the registrant to fill in a grid of data with details about marriage, sacraments, and, perhaps, ways to serve in the parish. That data goes into the computer as well, in all likelihood to sit there unused until a new staff person joins the parish and needs some information or until the disk crashes.

As an aside, let me say that I do seriously question the value of all this data-gathering we do in the church. On the one hand, it gives the impression that Catholics have little privacy and their relationship with the church is a cluster of brute details, some of them embarrassingly personal; on the other hand, parishes hardly use the data and, just as soon as it is entered, it becomes obsolete.

If our parishes see themselves as communities, however, then new parishioners are becoming part of a community. Their

entrance should have some of the marks of a community experience. Here are some possible directions:

1. Develop a welcoming ministry.

A group of eight or ten parishioners can form a "welcoming
committee" and involve the new registrants in a process that
helps them understand the new community of the parish that
they have decided to join (usually after having "shopped
around" for a while). Attractive sign-up cards can be placed in
pews or in a particular place in the back of the church. During
the celebration of the eucharist, these new registrants who have
just moved into the parish can be invited to stand; after worship,
they can be asked to fill in the sign-up cards. This also gives the
congregation a chance to greet these new parishioners. (See the
next section for further ways the congregation can greet new
members.)

These sign-up cards, asking very basic information, can be
given to the parish secretary to begin the process of data-entry
(one wouldn't want to lose the names and addresses) and then
passed on to the welcoming committee. The welcoming committee would, first of all, call the new registrant and welcome them
in the name of the parish to the neighborhood, asking if there is
anything they need. Secondly, the welcoming committee can
make an appointment for a short visit with the new registrant.

The short visit of the welcoming committee has an apostolic
objective: to involve the registrant in their new community of
faith. It might have the following elements:

a. Welcome. The committee brings a warm word of welcome
from the parish; this can be represented by some kind of simple
gift from the parish, even the parish roster or its pictorial direc-
tory.

b. Information. The committee can bring information about
the parish, its services, educational resources and ministries.
Such information should be attractive and readable.

c. Data-gathering. The committee can help the registrant fill
out the necessary data the parish wants. It is important that the

parish not ask for any information that it does not need or will not follow up on.

d. Needs assessment. The committee can then ask if there are any special needs or services the new registrant seeks. This might range from educational resources to a sensitive exchange about a person's relationship with the church. Such needs, once gathered, should be passed on to respective ministries in the parish. For example, religious education can follow up on a registrant's desire to enroll children in school or the catechetical program; the social concerns ministry can follow up on any financial needs.

e. Invitation. The committee should invite every new registrant into ministry. This means not only noting the areas where people might want to serve, but making sure that parishioners actually invite people to serve in the areas of their interest. (Naturally, some discernment will follow upon this initial contact.)

f. Prayer. The committee can conclude its visit by praying with the newly registered people, perhaps asking if they have special needs or concerns that they would like mentioned in prayer.

Such a process could mean a lot to people who are joining parishes; it also gets them recognized at least by the welcoming committee. It far exceeds what happens in most parishes at the present time. Here are other ways a parish can amplify even this process.

2. Liturgical celebration of entrance into a parish.

If joining a parish means joining a community of faith, some faith celebration of the community makes a lot of sense. This need not be enormously elaborate because the new registrants are, after all, members of the Catholic Church! Our church is not congregational in its essence and, were we to become primarily congregational, we would lose our sense of being Catholic. However, a parish could design a simple rite of entrance to bring newly registered parishioners into its community more humanly and communally. What might this rite look like?

a. Designate one eucharist every month or every quarter as a "new parishioners' mass."

b. Through RSVP (the welcoming committee could handle this), determine who will attend.

c. At the greeting that begins the mass, the celebrant can call the names of new members and have the congregation acknowledge their presence (i.e., have the congregation introduce themselves to each other, including the new members, or even have the congregation applaud).

d. After the homily, the celebrant can ask the new members to come forward and, extending his hands, say a prayer over them. The following suggests what this prayer might be like:

> Lord, God of all humanity and God of every heart, you have desired to gather all people into a community of faith. Your call to our Jewish ancestors began this gathering, as you formed them into your chosen people. Your call in Jesus extended this gathering to every race and people and way of life.
>
> We, as a parish community, have become part of this gathering process, for you have made us your chosen people through baptism and you form us into unity through our celebration of faith in the eucharist and in the other sacraments.
>
> We thank you this day as we welcome new members into our parish community. We ask you to enrich their lives through their involvement with us, even as we expect to be enriched by their joining our community. We ask you to strengthen their faith through their involvement in our parish community. We ask you to help them, by their joining with us, to be your witnesses in today's world.
>
> We pray this through Christ our Lord. Amen.

e. At the end of mass, the new registrants are called up a final time. A simple gift is given them. It might be a parchment with the parish's mission statement or some other sign of the parish's spirituality.

A reception after the mass can conclude this liturgical celebration. Such a ritual will not add too much time to the celebration of the mass and it will signal to people who go through it their membership in the parish community.

3. A reception of welcome.

Parishes can also offer a reception of welcome. A hospitality or welcoming committee can take on this ministry as part of its service. Depending on the size of the parish, this can happen monthly, quarterly or bi-annually.

a. Newly registered people are invited to a reception with an RSVP.

b. The parish calls these members to remind them about the reception.

c. A somewhat elaborate reception is planned: juices, other beverages, fruits, finger-foods and even a simple meal, presented with tablecloth and candles. We want to say to people they are special.

d. Staff members and parish council members mingle with new registrants, keeping an eye out for those who seem to be hiding in the corner.

e. After the refreshments, the pastor and staff people introduce themselves; the parish council president introduces some members of the council; each gives a very short description of what he or she does in the parish.

f. Some information about the parish and opportunities to enlist in various ministries are arranged on a side table; the pastor or parish council president encourages people to take these.

Any or all of these processes can help parishioners feel that they have a special stake in their new parish. Elements of welcome such as these can reshape the basic image of our parish communities; through activities like these, they might come to see themselves as welcoming communities.

New Arrivals in a Neighborhood

Moving is a major characteristic of our society. Most families will have packed up and moved into a new town as many as five times. With every move, the connection between the family and a believing community grows more precarious. The associations, the friends, the special sacramental moments, the particular spirituality of a congregation get ripped from the family's experience. Will the next parish be the same as the last? Will they be as welcoming, as accepting, or as bored or picky as the last?

Just the very process of uprooting and resettling seems to induce tenuous relationships with church. Sociologists and statisticians rank "moving to another town" as one of the major reasons people are not involved in a church today. When we think of more settled patterns of town-living or urban-dwelling and the role the local church played in the past, it's no wonder that, taking these stable patterns away, the church simply does not play the same role. It's much harder for the local congregation to concentrate peoples' experience—and for people to focus themselves on the local congregation.

This makes it all the more essential for churches to have welcoming strategies for people who move into their areas. These strategies can take on two forms:

a. Neighbor watch

Our parishioners should be trained to watch when someone is selling or buying a house, or vacating or renting an apartment. They already have a natural curiosity about these newcomers. People are always wondering, "Who's moving in" and, "What will they be like?"

Our parishes should have "welcome packets" that parishioners can get at the back of the church. With these packets, they can approach new residents with a note of friendship and begin forming a relationship with them. The packet can give a parishioner a reason to visit with a neighbor and possibly begin involving that neighbor in a parish. This packet might contain:

1. a general brochure about the parish
2. a particular brochure about the school or religious education program
3. a booklet about your particular city or neighborhood
4. a list of convenience or emergency numbers
5. a listing of all the local churches and synagogues

6. a recent parish bulletin
7. a little memento of the church that people can keep at hand (telephone book, refrigerator magnet or calendar, for example).

Parishioners who welcome new residents should be advised to make the visit strictly "neighborly." A visit does not give parishioners a right to pry or snoop on people. A discreet question about whether they'd like information about local churches or, "Are you looking for a place of worship," is all that someone needs to invite people to share as much or as little as they want. Parishioners who do not live in the neighborhood of the parishes where they worship can likewise be on the lookout for friends and coworkers who seem to have no place of worship.

If parishes want to institute this kind of ministry and awareness, they can accomplish this with a few simple orientations near the dismissal part of a liturgy.

b. Neighborhood visiting

A parish might be more ambitious and deliberate by organizing home visits to new developments. This makes particular sense in fast-growing suburban parishes or in urban parishes where buildings have been "co-oped" and a new population has moved in—although actually entering urban apartment buildings might be a formidable challenge, given the level of security residents often demand.

A "neighbor visit" can be accomplished without an enormous strain for a parish. The first step would be to map out the sector of the parish that it wants to visit, copying down the numbers and streets (or apartment sequence). Figure that each team of two will visit twenty-five or thirty houses. Therefore, if there are 300 units to be visited, one will need at least twenty parishioners to agree to visit.

People will do this if they are told that this will only take six hours of their time over a one-month period. Two hours will be spent in preparing, training and assigning the units to be visited. Four hours will be spent visiting. This usually is sufficient time, because rarely will one find more than sixty percent of people at home. Of those found at home, most of the visits will be pleasant "social calls." Perhaps one or two families out of the thirty that a team might visit will actually get involved in a longer exchange.

The visits can have the following simple structure:

a. Greeting and introductions
b. Presentation of information about the parish.
c. Asking if the family has yet found a place of worship.
d. Asking if the family has any questions for the visitors.
e. Offering to pray with and for the family's needs.
f. Leaving some kind of simple gift or memento of the parish.

Although none of this will bring hoards of people into a particular church, it will accomplish certain things:

—it will give the Catholic families who are new a point of reference for your parish
—it will give witness that your parish is concerned and neighborly
—it will allow people who are making religious transitions to ask questions and begin a conversation with representatives of your parish
—it will instill and deepen a welcoming dimension for your parish.

Welcoming Those on the Inside

The final issue of welcoming is actually the most embarrassing because it concerns the kind of welcoming we do inside our own parishes.

Parishes have an "articulated structure" that can be put down on paper. The vision statement, the goals, the organizational structure and the lists of ministers and activities are examples of this. Beneath this, however, there is a more important "unarticulated structure" that actually runs the parish. This is the way parishioners make other parishioners feel. It deals with warmth, community and power. It emerges from the history of a parish blended with the kind of personalities that a parish attracts or rewards. These combine to forge the dynamics of a particular community—dynamics that can be particularly unwelcoming.

In virtually every parish that I've served or surveyed, the same scenario gets sketched: a small core of highly dedicated people who feel overworked and unappreciated and a large group of people who seem just to be "looking on." The small core insists that it's time for them to get help from the larger group, insinuating that this group is lazy or apathetic. The larger group, however, reports that when they offered to help or serve, "no one called us back."

Sad to say, those who have turf have a vested interest in keeping others off that turf. This, briefly, sums up the dynamics of many organizations in society—and also most of our parishes. True, some of this probably is unavoidable, with people reading signs of unwelcome where no signs are given. Some people inevitably seem like "insiders" to others. Still, this cannot explain such a widespread feeling of people being left "outside" the mainstream of the parish.

However we feel about it, the truth remains that if we cannot be welcoming within our own parishes, how can we be welcoming to others who are not members of our parishes?

Pastors need to challenge people in ministry to cultivate new ministers; indeed, this should be a criterion for continuing in ministry. If a minister cannot recruit another minister, that minister or committee member should be asked to step aside for a year or so. Pastors can also begin regular rotations of ministries. While most ministries are supposed to have a term-limit, by and large inertia dictates that we'll be happier just duplicating the assignment lists we already have than recruiting, training and assigning new people. Perhaps the resources used to involve new parishioners, spoken about above, could be utilized to periodically review seemingly "inactive people" in a parish. A decent goal would be that every family have at least one person involved in ministry in a parish.

Somewhat easier to organize, in terms of welcoming those who already belong to our parish, is some system of greeters for Sunday mass. It's only because we presume that our parishes exist only for "our own members" that we have no way of greeting people who come. Yet in every parish, at virtually every mass, there is always someone "new" or not a regular member.

We give scandalous example to these "irregular visitors" to our parishes. Our churches are cold and sterile. No one helps orient people. Ushers are wandering around, moving money bags, boxes of candles or having a cigarette on the side. Visitors for the first time enter an empty building and "fend for themselves." No one helps them find song-books or other worship resources. We can just imagine how much untold energy a stranger to our church must expend trying to guess what the assembly will do next (sit, stand, kneel, sit) and why.

If we can simplify our worship structure, greet people as they come in, have people greet and meet each other when they arrive and make explicit why congregations are standing or sitting, we can alleviate a lot of this anxiety. It is no effort for celebrants or commentators to invite people, appropriately, to "Please be seated for the readings," or "Please remain standing for the prayer."

For all those people who might be attracted to Catholicism because it seems strange or arcane, far many more will be attracted because it represents God's formation of a community of people who welcome, celebrate, pray, invite, involve and serve.

We need no miracle to move in this direction. We need only to recognize what our parishes are about.

6

Evangelization and the Rite of Christian Initiation of Adults

The experience of conversion and entry into the church used to be somewhat private. In those parishes that provided a ministry for those who wanted to join the church, the priest would talk to the "prospective convert" in his office over several months in a series of personal sessions. When he judged the person was prepared to join the church, he would baptize that person or receive his or her profession of faith, usually in a chapel, either with or without a mass, accompanied by a few close friends and the sponsors.

In parishes that provided no such services, conversion was almost invisible. The priest would send the "prospective convert" down to an "information center" or "instructional center" where another priest or religious instructed the person over a series of months. At the end of this series, the person received baptism or made a profession of faith, usually at the center of instruction. After that, the person would start receiving the eucharist at his or her local parish, simply by appearing one Sunday as an almost invisible "new Catholic" or "convert."

In each case, the parish hardly knew its new converts and the converts hardly knew the parish. In each case, conversion was a private thing, done through the auspices of a willing pastor or willing agent, accomplished in the privacy of a person's soul and the chapel where baptism occurred.

Parishioners, then, never saw conversion happening. They never celebrated conversion. Catholics never connected the awesome transition from non-belief to belief with their own worship or faith life. The community never reflected on itself through the experience of those who were joining the church. It never officially greeted people who were joining the church nor did it have a way for those people to begin feeling at home in their new church.

Whenever parishioners begin to greet and welcome each other (an all too rare occurrence in many parishes), one of the most embarrassing moments occurs when a convert, standing up in the group, meekly says: "I joined the church as an adult and it was three or four years before I felt comfortable; even now, I still do not feel completely accepted." When I've heard this said, it is not done with rancor or even regret, just as a matter of fact (and as a mirror to the way we Catholics so often are).

The welcoming and greeting that we have been so poor at was magnified even more by the conspicuous absence of any public welcoming gesture to those who, often at great sacrifice, had decided to join the church. Here are people giving their lives and making commitments to Christ in our church, and yet we have such a hard time even adequately welcoming them.

A Public Rite

The Rite of Christian Initiation of Adults brought all of this out of its secretive privacy. In doing so, it made conversion an issue for the church and for every parish. Conversion is in itself a complex issue we shall be discussing later; but at least Catholics can begin to sense its complexity through their parish and worship.

Year by year, parishes which have begun celebrating the rite have seen men and women, old and young, presented before the congregation. Year by year, they have seen these people led out of mass by someone holding high the book of the gospels. Year by year, they have been invited to meet these people; their names have appeared in announcements; and their bodies have been doused with water, for everyone to see, at the Easter Vigil.

While initially parishes felt awkward about these practices, particularly about sending people out of mass to explore the word of God while the rest of the congregation stayed for the continued eucharist, parishes (and those going through the various initiating rites) have gradually come to feel comfortable about them.

More subtly, as the Rite of Christian Initiation for Adults has taken hold of various parishes, tens if not dozens of ordinary Catholic parishioners have become involved in the process itself, as sponsors or in other capacities. This has given them not only a vested interest in the persons who are undergoing conversion, but also in the conversion process itself. Before this, only a handful of forward-looking instruction centers or parishes actually involved lay people in the work of helping others join the church. This kind of work belonged to priests or, maybe, sisters. (The mentality flowing from this practice has continued with a vengeance into our own day. Catholics routinely will not see evangelization as something that *they* do or have a part in. As soon as an evangelizing moment arises, many Catholics choke. It's "send them to Father," or "call in the expert"—with disastrous consequences for the church as an evangelizing community.)

Because the rite has made the process of entering the church public, right there for everyone to see, it has also raised the question of conversion for the *whole parish* community in ways that cannot be avoided. When parishioners see men and women leaving the assembly to reflect on the word, they have to ask themselves: why are these people joining the church? What do they see as so valuable in it? Why are these people experiencing change? What must that change feel like?

Inevitably, this raises questions for the observing parishioner: how am I experiencing change? What do I see of value in my church? Do I prize the church, my faith, the way these people prize it? What change is God calling me to undergo? In what way do I have to be converted?

Ultimately, Catholics will have to understand themselves as a converted people. Only when that comes about will Catholics typically, as part of their Catholic life, invite others to conversion.

Steps toward Faith

The catechumenate forms a process of initiation in which people experience conversion. The steps of the process mirror the development and maturity of the faith of people passing through the process. Each developmental period receives a special rite to signal its completion. We can display these periods and rites as follows:

PERIOD	RITE
Period of evangelization, and inquiry which is completed through entrance into the catechumenate.	Rite of Entrance into the Catechumenate.
Development of the catechumens' spirituality through prayer, reflection on the scriptures, study, discussion and faith sharing.	Rite of Election.
Preparation of the catechumens for baptism, confirmation and eucharist at the Easter Vigil (usually during the period of Lent).	Rite of Initiation (reception of baptism, confirmation and eucharist, usually at the Easter Vigil).
Period of mystagogia, continued maturing as a disciple and member of the church.	

This process, with its steps and rites, forms a rhythm through which a person directs him or herself toward initiation in the church. The rhythm has times of preparation, study and discovery; these times may take longer or shorter, depending on what is happening in the life of the individual. These times reach a climax with the celebration of the various rites, with each rite asking a deeper commitment and a clearer direction from those who are preparing to enter the church.

What the rites do, then, is clarify the spirituality of the person. At different points in our lives, we might see ourselves discovering certain truths or growing in certain ways. How do we know this is really happening? How is it verified in our lives? How do we separate the fantasies we have about ourselves from the true directions that are taking hold in our lives?

To do this, we need signs, both the human signs that we receive from others who can affirm or question what we say and do, and the symbolic signs that relate us, profoundly, to a community of believers. When I see water poured on someone, when I smell the perfumed oil, when I watch people signed with a cross, when I see them receive the book of the scriptures, then I know in a different way what is going on inside that other person and how that person is becoming connected to me, as a believer, and to our faith community.

Essential Contributions

The Rite of Christian Initiation of Adults has clarified many elements of conversion and entrance into the church; in the relatively few years of its adoption, it has made essential contributions to key ideas of evangelization.

1. *It has rejected a solitary notion of conversion and evangelization, insisting that the process of turning to God always take place in community.*

It has become so easy, especially in the English-speaking North American world, to think of conversion as a personal decision one makes toward God through some acceptance of Jesus as "my personal Lord and Savior," that the fact that conversion takes place in the context of the people Jesus formed, inspired, and continues to animate has become completely lost. Of course, people convert not to the church but to God; yet, a God, or Jesus, apart from the reality of church, of a gathered people, simply is not the God or Jesus of the New Testament.

2. *It has shown how religious experience is verified through communal experience with others.*

The "reality" of the church is also the "reality check" of the church, namely, every significant internal transformation that happens to a person will be reflected in, and reflected back by, other people. Marvel as we might about great changes inside us, those changes mean nothing until our relationships with others also change. And they mean little unless they endure to become part of who-we-are.

3. *It has also made clear that conversion is not the "end point," but the starting point of a relationship with Christ.*

The initiation rites presume a journey. That journey may begin with inquiry or curiosity; it must include a radical turning to God; but it must also proceed beyond that, into discipleship, into the ongoing searching of God's word with other believers and the celebration of God's redemption in the eucharist and the serving of others in all their areas of need. In this way, it does not make conversion the final goal but an essential step. It keeps "final" things where they belong, in the experience of God after this life.

4. *It demonstrates that conversion is multilayered and continual.*

The process of joining the church entails steps, climaxes and plateau levels, followed by further steps, climaxes and other plateau levels. This puts an enormous dynamism into the exercise of Christian life, inviting believers to assume that their present relationship with God and with others can—must—expect further growth. It gives the church the leverage to continue to expect conversion from its members as much as it gives members the right to continue to demand conversion of the church.

5. *It shows the importance of ritual.*

Each step of the conversion and initiation process has its ritual celebration. That ritual action does more than give liturgists a reason for their jobs. It forces the catechumen to appropriate the development that has happened inside him or her. It also ties that catechumen into the community because the ritual experience touches not only the one being initiated but the whole community as well. In doing this, it demonstrates the full humanity of Christian faith, touching the body as well as the spirit of people. Ritual externalizes the spiritual actions and assumptions of everyone, drawing into one, through observable experiences, all the different people that make up the community. All see, all feel, all acknowledge and all are moved by the ritual experiences.

6. *It allows those being initiated to serve the church.*

As soon as they are catechumens, those contemplating entrance into the church have begun serving the community of believers by their presence, their witness, their questions and inquiry. People immediately have a place in the church; just as immediately, they have impact on the congregation. The community sees these people in the sanctuary; it can talk to them about their desires, hungers and experiences. It can befriend these people and be touched by the conversion they are undergoing.

7. *It gives us a more nuanced idea of membership in the church.*

Catechumens, even before baptism, belong to the community. Although they cannot receive the eucharist or many of the other sacraments, they can both marry in the church and be buried from the church. They are also welcome to stay in the catechumenal state as long as it makes sense. This graduated membership may well make more sense as we no longer have homogeneous Christian communities in which "everyone is Catholic" or Christian and as we continue pondering what the baptism of children means in terms of the Rite of Christian Initiation of Adults. Maybe we can broaden our concept of church membership, having space for more people who are testing the waters or going through issues instead of a uniform concept of membership that allows no subtleties.

8. *Lastly, the initiation process has tightened our notion of conversion and made us ecumenically sensitive.*

It wasn't many years ago when a tremendous stir arose in the United States because the Episcopalian daughter of the President of the United States was baptized (albeit conditionally) upon entrance into the Catholic Church. Such an attitude reflected the "non-Catholic" syndrome completely: all who were non-Catholics were the same, be they atheists, Hindus, Jews or Anglicans!

Such insensitivity to the Christian faith of others and such a demotion of the value of baptism has been eliminated by the distinction between "convert"—which applies to unbaptized people who join the church—from "candidate"—which applies to people baptized in other Christian traditions who decide to enter into full communion with the Catholic Church. Candidates are welcomed into the church. They are not considered converts. Their evangelization has already begun and they have already had a relationship to the church, even if inadequately, through another Christian group. The grace of God in Jesus has already operated, in a clear way, in their lives and the initiation rites respect this. In fact, candidates do not usually go through the full process that was outlined above.

These contributions to the idea of evangelization and conversion have permanently benefited the church. Not only does the church initiate people better today; perhaps more importantly, the church has a better idea of itself because of the initiating rites.

Evangelization's Contribution

Evangelization, with its distinct perspective of invitation, welcome and concern for those who are not members of the church, has a lot to contribute to the practice of the Rite of Christian Initiation of Adults. Because the emergence of this rite in recent church practice will undergo gradual maturing, evangelization can help it mature well by calling attention to the following issues of potential concern.

1. *Evangelization asks the ministry of initiation whether their sweep is broad enough.*

When people first think about joining the Catholic Church, the Rite of Initiation is explained to them. To so many, it seems like too much. First they may well be asked to wait until the next Fall or until some other period before they can begin the process. Next, it may seem like endless classes, exchanges and rites—when all a person wanted to do was "join the church." Sometimes people are asking for even less than full initiation and it seems like "too much." I heard the story of an adult who wanted to complete baptism by receiving the sacrament of confirmation who, even after his second year in the catechumenal process, was judged not "ready" and asked to spend yet another year in the process. Grace may be subtle, but perhaps we can be a little more generous in presuming its presence.

In other words, the catechumenal rite can come across as being judgmental and, backhandedly, as even denying grace because it can take on the flavor of Boy Scout "merit badges," as catechumens and candidates progress from stage to stage. Rather than a gracious way to welcome people and help them enter the church, it can appear as an ungracious, even a hostile, obstacle course. While the best ministries of initiation avoid these pitfalls, some do not.

One of the evangelizing patterns of the New Testament seems to have been that of throwing a wide net and letting Christians sort themselves out later. What else can be the meaning of the parables of the sower and the seed, or the weeds and the wheat, or the dragnet? The kingdom initially attracts a whole range of people who, upon entrance, find themselves distracted; judgment will eventually come to these people, but in time. (Scan the parables in Matthew 13 from this point of view.)

The Rite of Christian Initiation of Adults, then, has to embody the openness and compassion that characterize the New Testament; the framework of evangelization can help maintain this open vision.

2. *The Rite of Christian Initiation of Adults has to let people be in the place that makes sense for them.*

The process of the initiation rites brilliantly serves the pace of the individual candidate. I've seen people helped by the process to know they were not ready for full initiation. I've seen many people who appear to have experienced enormous spiritual and personal growth through the stages of the rite.

There is, however, more than a tendency to put into the group of those being initiated everyone who does not fit the category of "fully practicing Catholic." Mixed into this group will be evangelized Protestants seeking full communion, evangelized Catholics who have issues or difficulties with one or another aspect of church teaching, or partially evangelized Catholics who have "been away" or who have "forgotten" their faith. This is a natural tendency since, having arranged the formidable ministries and preparations to organize the catechumenate, pastors feel it should serve the greatest numbers.

However, such practicality does not take into account the true purpose of the rite (to complete the evangelization of unbaptized people), nor the different situations that some people find themselves in. Evangelized Protestants, seeking full communion with the church, should be insulted if they are directed to the group preparing for initiation into the church. They are already initiated! Such practices not only diminish the faith that other people authentically have but also blind parishes and ministers to the diverse ministry they should be providing for people.

Perhaps some creative use of the inquiry phase, prior to the Rite of Christian Initiation of Adults, with a specialized ministry for those who have already been initiated, can better handle the theological and pastoral problems that arise from putting everyone into the same group, irrespective of their category.

3. *Evangelization can help those who minister in the Rite of Christian Initiation of Adults to more greatly value what happens before people actually come to the church for initiation.*

In most parishes I've observed people trained in liturgy supervise the Rite of Christian Initiation of Adults. They are specialists in liturgy, very often in music, with a strong suit in aspects of theology needed for their liturgy degree. What happens around and in the sanctuary constitutes their primary concern.

However, in actual life people seek entrance to the church only after they have been touched and influenced by ordinary Catholics in settings usually far away from the sanctuary. They observe Catholics at work, or they are neighbors, or their children play with Catholic children, or they have sent their children to Catholic school. These are not areas that liturgists necessarily know how to capitalize on so as to invite people into the initiation process.

How often, for example, are candidates for the rites of initiation sought by a message in the bulletin? After one or two years, fewer candidates appear and pastors wonder why? Is it not perfectly obvious that the Rite of Christian Initiation of Adults depends on very wide evangelizing strategies in order to continue its ministry? Yet those involved in initiation often stand apart from direct evangelizing efforts, leaving them for the "team" or an extra-zealous lay person or priest. While hostility rarely exists between initiating and evangelizing ministries, non-cooperation often is typical. At the same time, it is usually the ministers of the rite who have both the professional staffing and the budget, so a greater stretching on their part makes the most sense.

4. *Evangelization asks those who direct the Rite of Initiation whether they are assuming that the rite's patterns are the fundamental patterns of Christian life, and whether this assumption has merit.*

After all, it is logical to say that because the Rite of Initiation is the normative way of adult conversion and adult conversion is at the heart of church experience, then everyone who is an adult believer should have passed through something like the Rite of Christian Initiation of Adults. In other words, the argument would run this way: the rites are not only normative of Christian initiation, they are normative of Christian experience. Those ministering in the initiation process have both the assumption and the evidence that this process produces mature believers. Accordingly, the patterns of the rite appear not only to apply to those being initiated but also to the whole church. In fact, for many liturgists, these rites can become ways of changing the church, making the parish less formalistic and program-driven and more relational.

But what is the price of this kind of assumption? While it is clear that the Rite of Christian Initiation of Adults has many valuable contributions to make to Catholic life as a whole, it also seems clear that it tilts the scale toward adult conversion and away from the more widespread form of initiating people through the cultural processes of child-rearing and education. Whole categories of active, believing Catholics can tend to be dismissed because they have not passed through something like these initiating rites. (The same thing happens with specialized adult experiences of conversion like Cursillo and the

Charismatic Renewal—a subtle scorning of the "ordinary Catholic"—from a more elite position.)

The wide expression of salvation and conversion in the New Testament, however, should keep us from assuming that any "one way" is the "only" or "best" way conversion happens. (This will be discussed in chapters 8 and 10.) We should be sensitive to the conversion experiences that ordinary people actually undergo, even though in ways we do not usually acknowledge or celebrate.

5. *Evangelization also asks: what are people being initiated into?*

Anecdotal information leads me to suspect that many people, having gone through the process of initiation, stop practicing their faith not too long after they are initiated or received into the church. While a "recidivism" is always a danger with converts and while a percentage of people who came in through the old "inquiry" method also stopped practicing their faith, one suspects that the problem is greater with the renewed rite.

Actually the Rite of Christian Initiation of Adults is only that: a collection of rites with certain general directives for the processes that might lead up to or flow from the major celebrations. It is our liturgical, catechetical or even psychological creativity that has created our form of the rite in the United States. This leads to the question: *Are people being initiated into the rite but not into the church?* Are people being initiated into the sharing process, the small group, the support system, but not into the parish as a whole, or worse, into the church as a whole?

If we insist that parishes and the church as a whole should be providing the sharing and support people have found in the Rite of Christian Initiation of Adults, then we must be prepared to overlook almost twenty centuries of actual Christian history as well as the organization of most contemporary parishes. We should not be sacrificing candidates for the sake of being prophetic about the direction of the larger church. If people evangelized through the catechumenate will be expecting small support groups, then providing these becomes part of the ministry. This has to happen whether the parish as a whole forms these groups or not. At the end of the rites of initiation, the new

Christian should be prepared to live Catholic life both as it is and as it could be. In other words, the small group process, including prayer, discernment, support and learning, which catechumens experience as part of entering into the church, makes important claims on the parish community to continue providing some similar kinds of experience for catechumens after they are received.

6. *Lastly, evangelization asks how diverse the leadership and sponsorship in the process of initiation can be.*

Like most things in a parish, a group will emerge to take over or take charge of a ministry or process. Like most things in a parish, that group will soon have a stranglehold on the ministry or process. Unfortunately, when this happens with the Rite of Christian Initiation of Adults, the opportunity for many parishioners to experience themselves firsthand as evangelizers gets lost.

Leaders and especially sponsors of these rites should have a natural turnover, providing training for others who have been invited into this ministry. The privilege of journeying with another in faith should be extended as far as possible through the faith community. This, in itself, might help the Rite of Christian Initiation of Adults plug more directly into the larger picture of evangelization, making more Catholics able to invite others into the catechumenate because they have become sensitive to the ways of seeking and searching in today's society.

A Bright Future

The energy that parishes in particular and the Catholic Church in the United States have begun to feel through the adoption of the Rite of Christian Initiation of Adults is one of the greatest gifts of the Holy Spirit to contemporary Catholicism. Parishes in decaying inner cities and booming suburbs each have felt a "rush" as they have ministered to people seeking entrance into the church.

This energy accounts for the fact that the Catholic Church is one of the few growing mainline churches. The experience of conversion, with its invitation that everyone in the parish begin to experience conversion, is gradually registering in the minds of average Catholics. Converts narrate their journey of faith, evoking in active Catholics the story of their own faith journeys. Sponsors, learning to share faith with a candidate or catechumen, want to share faith with others. Congregations want to explore God's word as they see groups of catechumens leave the assembly every Sunday to do just that.

These are powerful ingredients that offer the possibility of a very bright future for the Catholic Church. Churches that do not evangelize, after all, are dying churches; having an active, sensitive and flexible ministry of initiation is one of the best ways to make sure that churches have a vested interest in evangelization.

7

Evangelization and the Mass

They're bored to death. We know it. We see them coming as late as they can, Sunday after Sunday, timing their departure from their homes to the prevailing traffic patterns, so that they can arrive after the music rehearsals, the introductory commentary and often after the first reading. We see them fidgeting with their watches if the homily goes beyond ten minutes. We note a look of desperation if there is a second collection which will make them stay two, maybe three, minutes longer. We see them exit from the side doors of the church with the communion host still in their mouths, heading off for donuts or golf.

They're bored to death, coming to mass on Sunday not exactly out of obligation (those types probably have died off) but more probably out of rote. This routine now forms part of their weekend ritual and, while they probably would not miss mass— unless it was terribly inconvenient—it certainly does not rank among the high points of their week or their weekend.

I am describing here our "average" Catholic churchgoer, the "person in the pew," and not the millions who don't feel any desire to attend worship on Sunday unless it's an unusual burst of religiosity or a special occasion. These millions, if they go to worship, probably are so much "in their own space" that they do not feel much beyond what *they* are disposed to feel—maybe they want some quiet time, or maybe something is bothering them. But they probably are not coming for the liturgy itself. If a modern, updated liturgy was supposed to attract these random worshippers, it surely has failed. It has, however, attracted and held the average "Sunday Catholic."

These "Sunday Catholics" love God. Sure, they wouldn't feel

right if they skipped worship. Sure, worship fills out part of their personal and social life. But more than these, God is *important* enough for them to go through the liturgical routine every weekend. They love God enough to show God has an immovable place in their lives and their weekend schedules. But, still, they are bored to death.

Naturally, we talk and write about things we should be doing to "make the mass less boring," usually with reference to teenagers or young adults (as if older people weren't just as bored). We look for articles and conferences on music or the homily which can excite people, involve them and make them feel less bored. We assemble mini-orchestras with a variety of sounds and tunes to entertain the congregation; sometimes people even sway to the music.

We might even get our preachers to go to workshops on preaching, discovering how to pack ten minutes with exactly the right combination of story and melodrama to keep a congregation from slipping into slumber after the gospel. Will not a good preacher have people smiling as he enters a pulpit or dabbing their eyes as he leaves? "You're so good, Father, you just know how to preach. You make us feel so good."

Yet even these efforts betray the problem. We can entertain people for a few moments with music or a few moments longer with stirring preaching. But we cannot break through their basic boredom which is the backdrop to their worship experience. Perhaps we can tease a few moments of relief from that religious dullness—that's the great, weekly ministerial task. Yet the boredom remains, with the moments of excitement being notable exceptions.

We have had almost one and a half generations to develop the "vernacular mass" as we used to call it. First we had mass basically facing the people, mostly in Latin, but with "the peoples' parts" in English. Then we had the whole thing in English, embarrassed as we were by the English translations of Romanized, over-stylized prayers that made hardly any sense to us (if they ever made sense to God). Then we had the liturgy re-tuned: new scriptural translations, new altar prayers, new (and varied) eucharistic prayers. Then we had commentators, lectors, musicians and eucharistic ministers. Slowly we have evolved the form that we now use across the face of western Catholicism. And the judgment? People are bored.

We might feel relieved that 55 percent of the people in the United States attend mass on a Sunday. We know these figures are higher than, for example, those in Montreal, in Paris and, dare we say it, in Rome itself. Maybe we are doing something right, to have practically the highest percentage of attendance at mass in the industrialized world, slightly better than even Protestant churches in the United States. Not bad, even granting it's unevenness—that urban attendance can be nearly zero while suburban churches are shuffling people between masses as fast as they can. Not bad, 55 percent.

Except that these, too, are bored. These are the ones we see. We note their yawns. We hear their lazy footsteps. We feel the pressure they put on us "to get mass over with."

What the Issue Is

The issue, however, is not really about boredom. Putting it that way lays too much on us. It forces us into the "entertainment" business, as if that's what Jesus did in Galilee two millennia ago. As if the saints of our church—Augustine, Catherine, Ignatius, or Elizabeth Ann—were in it for the entertainment. Were we to entertain people perfectly every Sunday, will we have accomplished our task as religious leaders? It certainly seems like the only cultural forms that modern Americans respond to in great numbers are entertainment and therapy, so much so that much popular religion has adapted precisely these two moods. But adopting these moods in our Catholic worship still will not get at the real issue.

What is the real issue? It is about something even more elusive, even more disturbing. What people have been signaling to us over these decades leads us to a very unsettling impression: at worship, they don't feel they have contact with God. Worse than being bored, people don't feel touched by God.

How else explain this crazy nostalgia for "the Latin mass" by people who were not born when the mass was said in Latin? Somehow they pick up the idea that when the mass was in Latin there existed a "sense of mystery" and "the sacred" which just does not seem part of the liturgy we have constructed over these past twenty-five years. Understanding the words and prayers is not what they are looking for. They want something else, something that helps them know that they are in contact with God.

You would think that our new liturgy would perfectly do that. Here it is, in a language they can readily grasp and an immediacy that's right in front of their faces. Here God's word is proclaimed with ever greater competence in church communities across the modern world. Here the eucharistic prayer is proclaimed or even sung (certainly not whispered) for the congregation, with its responses coming at regular intervals. We no longer need bells to orient us to what is happening. Here the eucharistic bread is held before their eyes, and the cup is given into their hands. Here are congregations receiving the body and blood of Christ every week. What more can people want?

They are telling us. They will go halfway around the world to Medjugorje to feel it. They will travel hours to see the apparently bleeding hands of a priest. They will gather in prayer groups and invent new vocabularies. They will lobby for novenas and will light candles before their favorite saint—at home, if they cannot do it in church anymore. They will do whatever it takes for them to have *a sense of contact with God.*

Because they are not getting that at our liturgies.

Maybe, we might think, it's because we've made things too busy for them. Open to this page, sing, stand, sit, stand again, sing again, now these words are spoken, now those lines are said, predictably one after another, Sunday after Sunday. If the word *liturgy* means "work of the people," we perhaps have overdone the "work" part.

Or perhaps, as I've heard it said, we've made it too relational for people—too much acknowledging neighbors and shaking hands and chatting before mass and talking about community. When this is said, my eyebrows generally rise in surprise since most Catholics I know, even when the emphasis is on community, hardly acknowledge the people with whom they've come to mass—say, their own family members—let alone anyone else in the congregation.

Clearly, the answer is not in the direction of eliminating the relational elements we have introduced into the liturgy with so much effort. We need not subscribe to a new dichotomy between "God" and "community" as if they were somehow mutually exclusive. Besides, many of the experiences which people claim bring them closer to God *involve other people,* as the phenomenon of Bible sharing and/or quasi-Pentecostal groups shows.

Whatever our particular diagnosis of the liturgy, the case can safely be put this way: people come to worship because they want "contact with God" and, by and large, they are not getting that.

Contact with God

It's a strange idea, "contact with God," because when we try to trace it down, there are obvious problems. Was it Hegel who said that God does not leave himself open for ordinary observation? We don't experience God the way we experience each other, or things, or the weather or our own moods.

So how do we experience God? Why should we attribute a certain set of feelings to "God experience" and other kinds of feelings to "ordinary experience" or "worldly experience"? Is God experienced more when people read scriptures than when they experience "nature" (as it is so often put)? Is God experienced more when I sing than when I listen? Is contemplation more "God experience" than action—as many centuries of Catholicism would be inclined to say? Do we think God has eyes, hands, a face that provide us with some graphic way to "have contact"?

Well, to be exact, yes God does! We call Jesus the eyes, hands and face of God. We confess Jesus is Lord because we believe Jesus brings us into the mystery of the divine. We acknowledge

Jesus as priest (though he obviously was not, in his historical life, any such thing) because he penetrates the "veil of heaven" to bring us access to God. We proclaim that the prophetic words about the nearness of God have been fulfilled in Christ and that, through him, they continue to be fulfilled in our lives.

If liturgy could present people with an experience of Christ, with contact with Jesus, it would come closer to what people are actually seeking today.

But, of course, that's what liturgy is all about, we say! It is supposed to bring us contact with Christ. What's the word read for? So we can hear Christ proclaiming and proclaimed in our assembly. What's the eucharistic food eaten for? So we can sacramentally be united with Christ. Why do we gather as a community? So we can experience Christ as his disciples.

How can people be so clearly missing the point that liturgy is bringing them exactly what they seek—a sense of contact with God through involvement with the person of Jesus Christ? If evangelization is a "big idea," which can shape and bring energy to a range of other religious concepts and movements, what can it bring to the idea of liturgy, particularly in the aspect we have sketched so far? What can it bring to the sense Catholics have of why they worship on Sunday and what eucharist means in their Catholic lives? How can it help them have contact with God in worship?

Evangelization and Liturgy

The dynamic of evangelization inevitably includes a pulling away and a rejoining. By "pulling away," I mean that it asks people to take a different perspective on their daily and ordinary life. It questions this life, judges this life and changes this life. It involves "good news" which, at the very least, means that the "news" is different from "past news" or the "old news" of our lives. It demands that the listener pull away from the place where he or she now stands, without denying his or her actual human experience.

"Repent, believe in the Good News," begins the message of

Jesus. (Cf. Mark 1:4 and Matthew 4:13.) "Repent" means to "turn your mind around." "Believe in the Good News" means to believe in the message Jesus is proclaiming, something different from all the other messages of his listeners' lives, a message about God's kingdom which is drawing near.

Clearly, Jesus is asking people to be in a "different space." Clearly, he wants them to change their lives around, to think and to act differently. He asks them to abstract from their present lives for the sake of new lives to come—the kingdom. Whatever Good News Jesus' listeners heard (and they heard it in a great variety of ways), whatever Good News God invites us to hear, it always involves a "pulling away" for the sake of something yet to come or now coming into our lives. Therefore, we cannot stay in the same place. Our minds, our hearts, our energies must go in other directions.

Yet after this dynamic of "pulling away," evangelization invites us to return to our life with the new perspective of the gospel. The test of being evangelized does not consist of mysticism or asceticism; it consists of service to the poor and doing what God asks of them. Notice how Luke introduces the "evangelizing" agenda of Jesus in chapter 4:16 ff. Jesus picks up Isaiah's scroll and attributes to his active ministry the signs of God's saving presence: the Lord has sent him to proclaim good news to the poor, bring liberty to captives, sight to the blind, escape to the oppressed, and to declare a time of mercy from God. Unless, it seems, Good News makes a difference in the way people live, it isn't that good.

Likewise in Matthew's gospel, would-be disciples can say, "Lord, Lord, we prayed in your name and cast out demons through you. We worked miracles." But the Lord will claim he does not know them. "Only those who do the will of my Father will be saved," says Jesus (Matthew 7:21–23). The test of the saved comes down to the giving of water to the thirsty, food to the hungry, clothing to the naked, comfort to the sick and company to the isolated and imprisoned (Matthew 25:31 ff.).

The dynamics of evangelization, then, invite Christians to come full circle—to pull back from their lives so they can rejoin those same lives with a renewed vision, a vision of God's coming kingdom.

These same dynamics are involved in eucharist. By emphasizing them, and the elements of the liturgy that support them, they can guide us toward a recovery of the power of liturgy today. Instead of watching a performance or going through a ritual or fulfilling an obligation, the eucharist, by emphasizing the "pulling back" and "sending forth" dynamics of evangelization, can begin to give people a sense of contact with God who, unless one "pulls away" in prayer, cannot be engaged in everyday life.

Christian Prayer

When we pray we instinctually pull back from our present space—the moment, the mentality, the preoccupations of our lives.

This pulling back, like the call of Jesus, forces us to review, judge and consider change in our lives. To be in God's presence makes us place our lives against the transcendent framework of absolute holiness, justice, peace and love. It sets our ordinary moments in stark contrast to the absolute moment of God's presence encountered in prayer. The historical experience of Jesus by his disciples was probably like this—a moment of contrast, of call, of judgment and decision.

This experience can be at first quite frightening because it seems to shake our lives' foundations. It judges and condemns so much of the shabbiness and emptiness of our hearts. It makes us tremble at the thought of the almighty One. It makes us stand in shame and sin even as it invites us from these. It makes us want to cast everything off for the sake of God. Remember Paul's cry: "I have judged all my past as rubbish for the sake of the one who called me" (Philippians 3:8).

Yet, what next? After these shattering experiences, which are not uncommon in Christian life, does it stop there, with a call to something like monasticism? Christianity has developed a monastic form of holiness which ably represents this "pulling away" from ordinary life. Monks, ascetics, in monasteries and deserts and mountains, all gave up their daily life and formed new associations, rooted in the renunciation of money, power and sex. Such associations were to announce to the world the freedom that God intended for it.

Yet the human race is not, as such, called to monasticism. Christianity ultimately does not invite us to escape life; rather than escaping it, Christianity invites Christ's followers to change and transform it. If some are called to renounce money, sex and power through monastic or religious life, Christians by and large are rather called to reshape money (so that justice may be done), sex (so that life and human relationship be valued as God values them) and power (so that all may be served). If Christians understand their lives only as a "pulling away," they have not addressed the meaning of the Incarnation or the full range of the proclamation of the kingdom and their experience of Christian life is incomplete. Even monastic Christians see their life as a way of helping the whole church fulfill its whole vision.

Prayer, then, demands that we pull back from our ordinary life; but it demands that we return to it, with a renewed vision and a Christian ethic that reflects God's involvement with our lives.

The prayer of the eucharist, then, should have these same evangelizing dynamics. Eucharist should have the same power in the lives of believers today as Christ had when he called the disciples to follow him. By the dynamics of call-and-response, Catholics should today be able to experience the God of Jesus.

Eucharistic Prayer

The thanksgiving that Christians do together in Jesus in their Sunday worship has the same call-and-response pattern of evangelization and prayer. It invites believers to "pull back" from their ordinary world and then to "rejoin it" as disciples. It does this by asking Christians to reaffirm their following of Jesus by responding to his word and identifying with his self-giving love. The elements of the mass from gathering, to singing and praying, through the reception of communion—all of which dramatize the call-and-response pattern of worship—should allow people to participate in the dying and rising of Jesus, the Paschal Mystery.

Yet is not all this obscured in the way we celebrate liturgy? People do not feel addressed; they do not sense they are being called and challenged; their response remains dull, muted and routine. Why? Why cannot liturgy be this evangelizing experience for which people long, an experience that brings them into contact with God, by pulling them away from their everyday life into a sense of transcendence, and then by empowering them to return to that same everyday life renewed and sustained? Why cannot the liturgy dramatize our share in the paschal mystery of Christ?

The structure of the mass, in fact, consists of dialogue and response, of calling and challenging, of responding and celebrating. It gathers people from their everyday lives into a celebration of word and sacrament that, having evoked faith and response, prepares them to return to their everyday world with renewed vision. It "pulls away" people from their "regular news" to hear "Good News"; it sends them forth as disciples once again confirmed in their experience of God through Jesus, the Spirit and the community of believers. The mass is an evangelizing event.

There is no reason why we cannot begin to emphasize some of these elements more clearly in the way liturgy is celebrated. Evangelization invites us to concentrate anew on the way we gather for mass, what people can experience there, and how they are sent forth. Here are a few suggestions about how, within present liturgical laws, evangelization can transform liturgy.

Entrance Rite

This rite, associated with people's entry into church, represents an actual pulling away from life's ordinary concerns. People have come to a different "space," often with different colors (the windows and altar decorations), aromas (wax, wine and incense) and sounds (music, common prayer). It begins with a greeting, a way for the celebrant to welcome people into this holy space and a way for people to welcome each other into this same holy space. Far from being a "distraction" to people's prayer, greeting and welcoming each other can be the precise way they enter into holy time and space of eucharist.

—People should greet each other at the start of liturgy.
—People should be focused on the celebration ahead.
—People should have quality time, at the entrance rite, to concentrate their mental and emotional energy on God, God's presence and love.

Instead of the hurried, haphazard "penitential rite" we do, this entrance rite can begin the "pulling away" that prayer, and evangelization, always entails by creating a threshold through which parishioners can pull away from the tremendous stress and busyness of modern life and enter "sacred space."

The entrance rite culminates in the opening prayer which again should give people quiet time to gather their minds to God. People do not have an experience like this at any other point in the week—a chance to stand, with the community of believers, with their minds (individual and communal) open to God. Is the way we *rush* into the opening prayer a sign of our own discomfort with the presence of God and the "pulling away" that this presence initially asks of us? We can make this threshold moment one of beginning to experience contact with God through clearer gestures and a time of silence.

Liturgy of the Word

Although more and more lectors are maturing in their ministry, the service of the word is, so often, just so many words coming at people. The word must have a focus—which, of course, it does have, in the conceptual unity between the first reading and the gospel. If we emphasize this focus, we can underline the *particular kind of call* that God's word is making to people at every eucharist celebration. This, in turn, allows parishioners to come to *a particular kind of response,* in faith.

—The first reading must be done with special clarity and emphasis.

How we process with the book of readings, how lectors engage
the congregation, and how the book is venerated not only brings
about this clarity; it also reveals the presence of Christ in the
reading of God's word.

—*People must use the psalm response to actually begin their
"response" to this first reading.* They need time to absorb that reading. The psalm response, which in the Tridentine mass was a
"gradual" song to fill in time until the gospel proclamation, is
really a collective way for people to begin responding. (It's not
likely that the tuneless phrasing of many of our responsorial
psalm musical settings actually permits this. Let's be honest
about how awful and uninvolving our communal singing is
because it is not conceived as simple, congregational responsive
singing, and this no more so the case than with the responsorial
psalm.)

—*The first reading is preparing people for the gospel. The second
reading should not become a distraction to this clear call.* Liturgical
law permits us to eliminate the second reading or even to put it
in another part of the mass; perhaps this should be more widely
considered in parishes today.

—*The gospel must be read in a way that brings people into the experience of Jesus, such that they cannot escape the import of his word.*
Avoiding over-dramatizing the reading of the gospel, priests and
deacons have the responsibility to drive those words into the
hearts of his hearers. If the proclaimer has lived with the gospel
throughout the week prior to Sunday, this will more likely happen because the words have been driven into his own heart.

—*The homily must continue this gospel experience, driving home
both the word and its importance, its demands, in for Christian living.*
The homily should call people to one or another form of conversion every time it is given. Homilies explore the scriptures precisely to evoke this kind of call to conversion, not to point out
elaborate verbal constructs or obscure rhetorical points. Of
course, if the homilist is not experiencing ongoing conversion,
the homily can scarcely have this quality.

—*The creed, then, is a faith response to the word.* Through it
believers say they accept that word; it is their "I believe."

Perhaps always using the wordy Nicene Creed obscures this; the Apostle's Creed or the renewal of baptism vows should be considered as alternatives. That creed should be the climax of the word service, like the reaction of the disciples to Jesus' teaching or healing.

The liturgy of the word should portray clearly through its emphases this call-and-response dimension, thereby setting up the call-and-response which the remainder of the liturgy evokes.

Liturgy of Eucharist

The liturgy of the eucharist represents, in ritual, the same dynamic as the liturgy of the word. It is an invitation to commitment and faith. It is a challenge.

As the gifts are gathered, the prayer calls people to center themselves in thanksgiving to God, the placing of their whole selves and lives in the hands of the Father, through Jesus and the Spirit. The trinitarian emphasis of the eucharistic prayer should remain clear; this is what reinforces the relational demands of Christian life—that we commit ourselves to each other and God in Christ Jesus through his Spirit.

For us Catholics, the consecration has always been a powerfully transcendent moment, an opportunity for wonder or adoration. No moment in the eucharist catches the "pulling away" experience of prayer as this time of adoration. Yet, for this reason, it has to be woven into the whole call-and-response pattern of the liturgy. If heads bow at the consecration, to what purpose? To lead us to commitment, to invest ourselves in the service of the kingdom.

This should be so clear that believers know, when they approach the table to receive, that they are accepting the way of life of Jesus, his consecration and self-giving death, as the pattern of their own lives. We eat his broken body; we drink his spilled blood. We share in his risen power by living as he lived. The eucharist allows no shortcut around the cross, nor any maudlin, sentimental evasion of the implication of the resurrection of Jesus. The eucharist brings us through Christ's paschal passage, through death to life.

—The memorial of the Lord's Supper should situate the congregation consciously before God in the presence of Jesus.

—The self-offering of the community with Jesus should be clear to all the worshippers.

—The "Great Amen" should seal people's identity with the self-offering of Jesus. Through it, people are responding to God with their whole lives, offering God "all honor and glory."

—The Lord's Prayer should express faith-filled trust which leads us, after the invitation to receive communion, to recommitment to Christ. Receiving the eucharist has to be the ultimate "altar call," an act of conversion and recommitment.

—The time after communion should be one of sacred presence, both individually and as a community, with God in Christ. Why is this time so cluttered and interrupted so much in our contemporary practice of liturgy? Are we so frightened of the presence of God? If music and spoken prayer can represent a valid response to receiving communion, so also can the stilled attention to the fact that God has, sacramentally, visited us in Christ.

Perhaps the varied use of music and silence, of kneeling and standing, during the eucharistic prayer can make the call-and-response structure of this part of the mass clearer.

Concluding Rite

Few are aware that the concluding rite is actually a commissioning. Yet any analysis of what *Ite, missa est* meant in the old Roman rite shows that this is exactly what this rite is all about. It empowers the congregation to go forward. It commissions them to return to ordinary lives with a renewed perspective. It sends them forth, not into an alien world, but into a world that God would love, consecrate and change through the everyday ministry of the disciple. Catholics do not see this in the way we conclude the mass, nor is their "Thanks be to God" a resounding acceptance of that commission. More likely, people are thanking God that finally the mass is over and they can get about other things they'd rather do.

—The final blessing and commissioning can be emphasized for what

it is. "You are sent forth," we can clearly say. "You are commissioned."
Only such a clear challenge makes sense of the eucharist itself.
Otherwise, it only remains a pulling away, an abstraction from
daily life, rather than a celebration of daily life and a recommit-
ted return to it.

Beyond Hiding

It is easy to hide behind the liturgy. It is so patterned, so pre-
dictable. Everything has been written out ahead of time, tradition looms large, expectations are not easily tampered with.
Instead of having to generate spontaneous and novel communal
experiences as so many non-liturgical congregations have to,
liturgy offers centuries of established patterns which have
shaped the spirituality of many parishioners (at least the ones in
the pews). Who would want to subject people to an arbitrary
array of gimmickry from which they have no recourse?

At the same time, the expectations of the liturgy can obscure
what liturgy is all about—a community gathered in prayer,
recommitting itself to God in response to the proclamation of
God's Good News and the presence of Christ Jesus in the
eucharist. Communities have dynamics, moods, gestures and
relationships; they cannot get along without these. So these
should not be suffocated behind the liturgy. Liturgy should
make these relationships clearer.

What I'm proposing here consists in no more than this: let
the actual structure of the liturgy do its job by streamlining some
elements so that the fundamental evangelizing highlights of liturgy can become clear to worshippers. This will bring about a
clearer set of dynamics which can help Catholics have some
sense of contact with God.

Of course, nothing prevents an even more radical approach
to certain parts of the liturgy—all permissible, of course—to
underline the sense of discipleship that liturgy calls for. Why
not, every now and then, have people share their reaction to the
gospel and to the homily in the pews with their neighbors? Why
not develop some ways in which lay people can motivate and

inspire other lay people (not to mention the clergy and staff) at some point during the liturgy? After communion, it would be easy in congregations small enough to actually solicit commitments to various tasks and needs the congregation foresees, so that the "Go, you are commissioned" meaning of the dismissal actually commissions parishioners.

We don't need to hide behind liturgy. We have gone beyond the *ex opere operato* formula well enough in these thirty years to begin risking something even more important. Sure, the liturgy works just by its being done. But how about helping the liturgy to work far more effectively by doing it from an evangelizing framework?

Given what people are signaling to us today, it probably wouldn't hurt.

Liturgy can do far more than entertainment and therapy because, instead of the self-centered dynamics of these moods, it offers people the liberating dynamic of centering their lives on God (rather on what God does for me). The paschal movement of dying and rising, of pulling away and rejoining, of call and response, is the revealed way by which people can attain God and begin to experience exactly what they are longing for.

8

Evangelization and the
Motives for Faith

The overwhelming majority of the 20,000 Catholic parishes in
the United States have all become, in recent years, entry points
into the Catholic Church. Although it was always true that people became Catholics through Catholic parishes, only the introduction of the Rite of Christian Initiation of Adults in most of
the parishes of the United States has changed them into *normal*
entry points into the church. Before this, people received
instructions from occasional pastors or priests who wished to
give them the time at the local parish, or else they were sent to
specialized centers of instruction.

As a result, people now enter the Catholic Church in thou-
sands of sites. In most parishes, Catholics hear from the pulpit
that the "RCIA" will begin soon and that candidates are being
sought. Rather than entry into the church looking like some eso-
teric act done in secret, parishes now celebrate initiation openly.

This gives us a much broader basis for asking and answering
an important question: What motivates people to enter the
church? In our own parishes we can begin to discover what
makes people open to evangelization and how they hear good
news today.

I am not asking a strictly "sociological" question because anyone who has helped another enter the church knows that the
prime causes of change are life's transitions. Many people will
think about becoming Catholic through the prism of marriage:
either they plan to marry a Catholic (a very frequent reason in
the past) or (more frequent today) they have been married for
years to a Catholic and now wish to join the church of their

spouse. Likewise, people may change religiously after the death of a spouse or parents; they now feel freer to pursue a notion they have long had but never felt they could act upon. A small percentage of them will be "changers"—passing through several churches during their lifetimes.

In this chapter, I wish to explore the more "theological" motives for evangelization, what people find compelling or powerful in the Catholic faith. In doing so, I will be elaborating an important and broad movement we have experienced in recent decades—the movement from "threat" to "value" as the primary motivation in the lives of many people today.

Threat

I was, as a Catholic, raised in a church that talked threat. In this, my experience lined up with the experience of many generations of Catholics. Our faith, awesome and overwhelming, made us afraid. We can explore the contours of this world that most Catholics over forty-five would have lived through.

All around us hovered dangers. Bad angels stood on our left shoulders, whispering those temptations we found almost irresistible. Above us, saints and good angels struggled hard for our souls, as well they might, given how easy it seemed for our souls to be forever lost. Beneath us loomed a vast hell, imprinted in our imaginations through mission sermons and the licking flames depicted in orange in the Baltimore Catechism. This hell, we felt, had to be crammed with poor, forever-damned souls.

After all, not only were most non-Catholics assumed to be in hell, most Catholics, when you really thought about it, were too. One went to hell for swallowing water before receiving communion, or receiving communion while in the ever-ready state of mortal sin, for sinning or even wanting to sin, for every erotic impulse, for ritual improprieties or unfulfilled obligations, for the taste of hamburger on Fridays and for oversleeping Sundays, for not supporting the church or sending one's children to Catholic school, for letting the host touch our teeth or letting our minds doubt the words a priest just articulated. These were

the popular constructions of our Catholic world. The result: one
went to hell very easily.

The church articulated a range of behaviors which were to be
enforced "under the pain of mortal sin," or, if this can be trans-
lated into how it actually functioned in our Catholic lives, "under
the threat of going to hell." Priests shuddered if they forgot the
last part of their daily obligatory prayers, nuns flinched if they
moved into too great a proximity to a male, children carried the
weight of all their parents who, having failed to go to mass, surely would be damned, and Catholics dreaded the loss of so many
of their non-Catholic friends who, because they could not accept
the plain, simple truth, might well spend forever in hell.

Every Saturday Catholics lined up by confessionals, uttering
their sins to an illuminated screen behind which a priest waited
to relieve them of a week's accumulation of guilt. While most
Catholics who received regularly repeated the same "venial" sins
("I lied, may have taken pleasure in impure thoughts, forgot to
say my morning prayers," etc.), still others looked to "make up
sins" to have something significant to confess. The whole proce-
dure was testimony to one massive assumption: that people
needed to confess weekly because they sinned seriously every
week, or most probably sinned seriously every week, or might
possibly have sinned seriously every week. While this ritual of
weekly confession had multiple causes in history and pastoral
practice, it basically enshrined the trilogy of guilt, fear and threat
into the heart of Catholic life.

What held this system together? What could make so many
millions of Catholics, over so many generations, believe that this
trilogy of guilt, fear and threat represented the heart of the New
Testament? First of all, this was not the whole story, because
Catholics experienced tremendous consolation and the joy of
sacramentally touching the divine itself; some Catholics simply
were not attuned to responding to threat. The very process of
confession produced the opposite: a sense of innocence
regained, of cleansing, or relief and, therefore, of salvation. The
very leaving of the threshold of the confessional's darkness into
the brighter lights of the church represented the crossing of a

spiritual threshold from impending damnation to the experience of salvific relief.

Secondly, this whole attitude of fear and threat served as part of a much larger pattern that was occurring during the years 1880–1960 in the United States: one of discipline, order, communal support and clear expectation. This larger pattern very much suited a struggling immigrant people entering a new society and was reinforced by a sense of disciple broader Protestant America supported as well. Threat helped us keep our lives together, our families united, and our noses to the grindstone.

Where Did It Go?

Quite obviously, the last generation and a half of Catholic life has seen a significant evaporation of the guilt-fear-threat syndrome. Catholics no longer walk around assuming they (or everyone else) will more likely go to hell than heaven. Even very conservative Catholics who wish a wholesale return to "the plain black and white truth" do not want a return to threat as the primary motivator of life.

Where did it go? What happened to that whole style of Catholicism?

The Second Vatican Council caused a change in the way truths of the faith were emphasized. While none of those truths was stricken from the catechism, some of them moved to the first chapters while others have moved further back. The direct reading of modern translations of the New Testament has opened up a better proportion of images of Jesus and his teaching than the fairly truncated set of images we Catholics digested before. Likewise, the lives of the saints ceased to be the basic way Catholics reflected on God's Good News. Rather, for over a quarter of a century, New Testament images have been directly heard by Catholic people.

Even more than this, however, the change in the social situation of Catholics had to impact on the kind of culture that Catholics needed for their survival. No longer an uneducated minority directly threatened by a hostile American environment, we no longer needed all that discipline to maintain our defenses. We could afford to relax, to not stay tense and wary all the time. We could afford to see that life, for all its risks and dangers, was probably pretty good after all.

Instead of a world in which grace seemed like a sudden bright speckle against an unbearably dark background, Catholics now saw a world wonderfully illuminated by grace pocked, now and then, by failure and sin.

It may well be that this optimism misreads both human life and the message of the New Testament, that life may be more pocked and scarred than many of us see it now. Even so, it seems clear that threat is not a prime motivator for faith. People will not be threatened easily or for long. Threats, in religion, work as well as threats in the household. The more one makes them, the more people feel they have to test them and the more they end up as set lines in a scenario rather than real communication.

One might argue an obvious fact: it seems that the religions growing fastest are religions that effectively threaten people. Fundamentalistic kinds of religions work by drawing sharp contrasts between the "saved members" and the "damned everyone-else." They tend to enforce this sharp contrast by referring frequently to hell and the ease with which one can go there (and the vigor with which God will send one there). Obviously, people find a no-nonsense religion attractive. However, it may just as well be true that these religions are getting exactly that percentage of the population who are capable of being threatened, who are susceptible to fear and insecurity because of the vagaries of their life stories. If this is the case, there will always be the ninety percent of the rest of us for whom threats no longer work as primary motivators of faith.

I came across a study of the practice of the faith in St. Augustine, Florida, in 1945. It went into a lot of detail about demographics (age, income, housing, etc.) as variables in church attendance, none of which concerns us here. What was most interesting was the obvious: mass attendance in 1945 was near 80 percent (now it hovers around 50 percent). At the same time, monthly reception of communion was at 43 percent! In other words, more people came to church, but more people came just to be there, because they "had" to. If fewer people come to church regularly today, probably as many (or more) of them really get involved in their faith in a personal way, living it less out of obligation and more out of a sense of participation in God's life. These past thirty years, in other words, may not be the simple loss that some people claim. [1]

New Motives

What these past thirty years since the Second Vatican Council have become is a vast laboratory in which we can study varieties on the motives of faith in today's world. Since the guilt-fear-threat trilogy has been in demise, with most of those people who depended on it dropping out of the church, Catholics have, in their actual church lives, discovered other, more compelling, motivations for their faith. Even more, they have been living these motivations out in their personal and church life for over a generation. And these motives have become the basis for others to enter the church.

In other words, there is religious life beyond fear and threat. I'd like to sketch out some of the themes that I've been over-hearing Catholics—those who have continued being active, those who are returning to the church and those joining the church—express. This sketch of motives does not obviously constitute a "new apologetic," since it lacks a full or encompassing theoretical expression. But it offers a look at religion more from the "value" side, the positive, than from the "fear" dimension which emphasized the negative. While not a "new apologetic," they point in the direction of one. I offer them as a list against which the reader can measure his or her own observations.

---

[1] George A. Kelly, *Catholics and the Practice of the Faith: A Census Study of the Diocese of Saint Augustine* (Catholic University of America Press, Washington, 1945).

HEALING

Catholics consistently speak about the experience of healing as important to their faith. Their faith has brought them deep peace and healing; the Catholic experience has brought them through some crisis or a set of key changes—this has resulted in a life that seems more whole and more wholesome.

The healing people speak about is not necessarily physical, much as we sometimes tend to think of religion in terms of miraculous healings (novenas) and much as many people still do (charismatic prayer groups). Nor are people referring primarily to healings that they experience, less miraculously, in the sacrament of anointing where people feel touched and healed by God, but don't run around the church throwing their crutches into the air.

Mostly Catholics seem to be referring to healing of a personal, perhaps psychological, nature. They point to life patterns that tended to be completely destructive of themselves or their families. They point to patterns of personal misery and depression. They talk about their greed, envy or lust. They paint dead-ends that they have encountered, wondering if they could ever escape. Their faith gave them that escape.

These are Catholics who fit what William James referred to as the "twice born," those who have been led, through a period of crisis, to see themselves anew. Not all of them may speak "born again" language, but they have, at root, the same experience of having the chance to begin life anew, to see themselves differently, to give up dead modes of behavior and find the power to assume life-sustaining modes of behavior. They have been healed. Saints from Augustine to Francis Assisi, from Mary Magdalene to Dorothy Day, have undergone experiences like this in the Catholic Church. What Catholics are saying is that this kind of life-change, coming through faith, has become a more ordinary way for them to see themselves.

As the Lord Jesus, in his earthly ministry, performed powerful deeds of healing as a sign of the inbreaking of the kingdom and the nearness of God, so these kinds of signs of healing, albeit in more subtle form, provide powerful motivation for faith today.

Justice

I also hear Catholics talk about how their faith and church help them give their lives to better the lives of others, especially those who suffer injustices and deprivations. Announcing the Good News, which Jesus proclaimed in the tradition of Isaiah in a particular way to the "poor" (Luke 4:16 ff.) and gathering in a regular community for worship sensitizes Catholics to the needs of others. When they respond to these needs, they find their faith enriched and they are powerfully attracted to deepening it.

Catholics who are motivated this way sense something more cohesive than simple "do-goodism." They see a fabric of faith that stretches from the generous creation of God, which makes all people equal in dignity and worth, to the final vision of a humanity gathered in fulfilled joy. They "see" Christ "hidden" in those who hunger and thirst, in the infirm and imprisoned, as Matthew's devastating parable drives home (Matthew 25:31 ff.).

Some may feel that this motive is a bit less "religious" than others, since it's impulse arises from the direct human experience of people in need rather than from something that might be construed as more exalted or spiritual. Even so, it powerfully expresses what is a constitutive dimension of Christian life and it helps correct the somewhat "talky" view of faith that religious people often give off. Not all people articulate their faith verbally, nor do all people find meaning through verbal or psychological connections that make sense to them. A significant number of people simply "do" their faith, a doing which they find as enriching as a profound meditation or an emotion-filled prayer group.

Whether it is through setting up soup kitchens or organizing a shelter for the homeless, or ministry to deprived youth or working for renewed housing, or bringing the eucharist to the sick or driving elderly people to the hospital, or donating clothing to agencies or raising funds for overseas hunger, these kinds of actions powerfully motivate people to faith. When the bishops of the United States developed their plan for evangelization, they could not complete it without a third goal, that of working toward the transformation of humanity through deeds of justice and peace. In this, they were following an instinct that explains for many people what faith is about.

FAMILY

Yet a third area Catholics mention when they talk about the importance of their faith revolves around their families. It has something to do with "passing something on" to the children, a set of values or ideals which people have, over the course of their maturing, have found essential to their vision of life. Gone are the sentiments of religion as "forced down my throat" or something that we did "just because it was expected." Over the years, as adolescence gave way to even greater experimentation as young adults, on through the process of settling down to "one person" and a clear value-system, nothing has spoken as cogently in the lives of Catholics as has their faith.

As a result, they would not think of depriving their children of this set of values. Stripped of the guilt and the compulsiveness that often made Catholicism seem somewhat hysterical or over-drawn, Catholic parents have settled on the core, the operative kerygma, as something their children simply must have: God loves us, God shows that love in Jesus, God asks us to reflect that love in the way we live with and for others.

But parents, when they talk about faith this way, seem to want to express yet something more than what they pass on to their children, something more than a living tradition. They seem to want also to express something about their own family's meaning.

It's as if they are saying that only faith helps them understand themselves as a unit, as a group destined to be together, forming each other and affecting each other's lives, as a community of intense sharing, generosity and sacrifice. Husbands see in the Catholic faith something of why they want to continue giving themselves to the wives they have loved and married; wives understand their bondedness to their husbands through the faith they share and practice together. Parents see the sacraments not only as moments of their children's growth but also as moments of their families' growing together. The unity they feel gathered at mass, even apart from the fussing of babies and the sulking of adolescents, resonates with what they feel as a natural family unit. The weekly hearing of the scriptures and joining in the body and blood of the Lord weaves the family into deeper patterns of love.

This is all beside the fact that Catholic families, by and large, do not readily express faith at home apart from grace at meals (if that), even though recent popes have tried to see Catholic families as "domestic churches" where religious practice becomes part of a family's way of life and witness to others. Even before Catholic families have discovered this truth, they are already seeing something more subtle about their existence: that their faith speaks directly and radically to their human lives. This they find compelling.

It shines on their ordinary lives replete with stumbling gestures or incomplete arguments, their risks and embraces, their sacrifices and dreams. It shines through the bonding of marriage into the whole process of begetting new life, cherishing it and bringing it into the kingdom Jesus announced. Likewise, the patterns of everyday life reflect back with a poignant brilliance on faith, helping Catholics today see the point of believing even as they feel the point of living. Faith is a dimension of their family; their family is an essential dimension of their faith.

COMMUNITY

"People aren't joining the church because of dogma, but because they are searching for community." When a brother priest reported this to me, shortly after the introduction of the adult catechumenate in our parish, it made me look back on all those whom I helped in a previous era join the church by the so-called "inquiry method"—a four month series of classes on the faith. Sure enough, when I reflected on it, the observation seemed true of them as well. As cogent and closely reasoned as a presentation of the Catholic faith could be, most people were responding to some kind of attachment, some kind of a desire to be linked to others in faith.

The surprise may be that this is at all surprising. After all, so much are individualism and privacy extolled in American society today, so important people's "own space" and "personal journey," that the quest for community, of being linked to others, might well seem invisible. People aren't looking for community, we feel; they are looking for themselves.

The problem, however, is in this individualistic portrait of life, as if community does not exist before we become individualized, as if community does not support the unique kinds of persons we are, as if community is not implicit in the very way we go about organizing our lives. Robert Bellah and his companions documented this style of American life in the justly-famous *Habits of the Heart* (University of California Press, Berkeley, 1985) and spoke about the way religion could redress the weaknesses of this isolating autonomy. What they spoke about seems to be operating in the lives of many people today.

Very few factors in contemporary American life speak to the sheer need that we have of each other. Work often divides people, some to be winners, some to be losers, all to compete with others one way or another. Government mouths large words about democracy and national unity, but it seems quite remote from the lives of most (until around April 15th). Education brings people together into some kind of discourse, but it has sold its birthright as a community of wisdom for the porridge of "buying a career." Our universities sell themselves as a preparation for the competitiveness people will find in the marketplace. Sports brings us together on the most superficial of levels; the common cheer is all we have in common. (Actually, powerful human drama gets acted out on the field, reflecting incredibly profound sentiments, but this hardly gets recognized.) Neighborhoods mean nothing to people who lock their doors, build bigger fences, turn on louder alarms and gather together only to insure their property values.

Church, however, offers something different—the chance to be with people who are valued simply for themselves, beyond any commercial transaction or utilitarian purpose. As our parishes articulate the gospel with greater clarity, they challenge people to become involved with more than just "their own kind."

Parish after parish has undergone the drama of "others" moving in and gradually becoming part of community, enriching the whole meaning of community in the process. While ethnic parishes still exist, most of these have had to become something more to survive.

People have profound needs of each other, of understanding themselves in larger networks and gatherings, and no amount of self-preoccupation will exorcise this from the human spirit. Where can this kind of need begin to be addressed, or where can it be addressed as movingly, as around the table of Jesus, sharing his bread and his life?

Community may mean something intimate for some, or something hardly felt for another. Its need exceeds the feeling level. It comes built into who we are, for none of us can be anything without each other. That God addressed us as community and that Jesus would gather all people into his household has not been lost on people. They see in this, almost instinctively, the sign of God's presence and the missing ingredient of their lives.

New Motives

Perhaps, by themselves, healing, justice, family and community may seem obvious, platitudinous or even inadequate. Certainly, observers keener than I will overhear other motives for faith that stir the soul more powerfully.

What we need to recognize is the birth of a way of being Catholic Christians that has flowered over these past thirty years and which reflects in a clearer form the range of values that the New Testament articulates.

For all the times we find Jesus yelling at people or threatening them (mostly self-righteous Pharisees or in passages urging fidelity under the threat of persecution), we find him more often healing people, calling them to serve each other, pointing them to their ordinary lives as the sphere of their religious concentration and gathering people into a community where all are accepted and loved.

Of course, threat is part of our theological furniture. The inability to accept the risks of missing God's call is one of the great failures of our modern vision. People are blithe about God, God's call, God's demands. Catholics dismiss too readily the idea of damnation and the spiritual tragedies that mark so much of modern life. Modern believers often want to make gray what is clearly black or white, to smudge what is sharp and neat.

Yet damnation is not an exclusively future possibility; it is a present actuality and, when pressed, one has to acknowledge that the clearest signs of damnation that people experience today are the failure to find healing or peace, the massive unjust oppression that constitute so much personal and national life, the disintegration of our human bonds as families and even as human beings. In other words, the threats of Jesus can be verified by the decay of so much modern life. People are losing their "souls" by the way they live; they are losing their very selves. What could be more "hellish" and "damnable" than being resigned to our brokenness, tolerating injustice and suffering, bereft of community now and forever, unable to experience God's healing, reconciling and fulfilling love? Practicing Catholics are teaching us that their motives for belief are the way they are escaping the fires of an empty human life.

We Catholics have learned, in the communal biography of our church since the Second Vatican Council, how Jesus continues to live in our world and how his values can urge us more than his (or the church's) threats. In this rediscovery, not only have the motives of faith been clarified by the way we have come to live; even more, the face of Jesus has become clearer in our church.

9

Evangelization and Ecumenism

To a casual observer, no two religious movements might seem so mutually opposed as ecumenism and evangelization. Given the stereotypical understanding that average people have of each of these transforming twentieth-century movements, it is no surprise. Each of these movements, once reduced to mere caricatures of themselves, appear bound for direct collision.

Evangelization, or even the more popularly-construed term "evangelism," looks to many people like a slick marketing movement. Evangelization sells church and church membership. It finds out demographics, needs and impulses and carefully packages just the attractive set of ideas and activities to make for a growing congregation. Evangelism books abound with titles that sound like a Madison Avenue person overdosed on the book of Acts. "How Evangelism Can Make a Church Grow," or "Booming Gospel, Booming Churches," and other such hoopla'ed images.

In its popular stereotype, evangelism, thought of as an explosion of new techniques, each designed to produce a desired effect, aims to get people into a church. It's a market-place strategy, a way for churches to compete, for the fittest to survive, the quickest to thrive, the slickest to override all the others.

Evangelism appears to be, then, the opposite of cooperation. When people evangelize, they are at war, struggling, conquering: battling Satan (or whatever is construed to be the enemy; often enough for some groups, Catholics are thought to be the enemy) and winning souls for Christ. But what good are souls without bodies—without bodies that are sitting in our churches, contributing to our collection, and building up our modern idol of the super-church?

Diametrically opposed to this marketing image of evangelism stands the popular stereotype of ecumenism: relativistic, trendy, wishy-washy. All these churches cooperating, talking with each other, sharing their resources, blending their theologies along with their social courtesies, have gotten into an ecumenical framework which people often feel actually dulls their church's image. "All religions are the same," ecumenism seems to be saying. "Nothing makes any difference. What religion you are makes no difference."

As uncomfortable as religious conflict makes modern Americans (who prize pluralism and civility above everything), this caricature of ecumenism as mealy-mouthed courtesy makes people perhaps more uncomfortable. If it's all the same, if it's all going to come down to a "least common denominator" of a faith, if there will be no stance or substance, why not just let our bland, plastic civil religion take over, with people content to have some vague references to a "Force Beyond Us" and soothing language about being "sisters and brothers," in spite of it all?

To a casual observer, evangelism looks too strong and ecumenism looks too weak. They go in opposite directions. They contradict. They can never peacefully meet.

Historical Connection

Viewing evangelization and ecumenism as alien religious movements, however, reads history the wrong way. History, in fact, shows their vital connection.

Perhaps no evangelization movement has borne more fruit than the mission movements in Africa in the past century. Hundreds of millions of Africans have become Christian since 1880, Christians of every conceivable stripe. The Roman Catholic Church has grown enormously, as have the mainline Protestant churches, with Africans becoming Methodists and Anglicans, Presbyterians and Baptists. At the same time the religion of Islam has swept through much of Africa as well. This vast continent's introduction to western life came through the two great children of Judaism, Christianity and Islam.

Yet along with the evangelizing energy of so many missionaries on the African continent, there grew the disturbing realization that this very missionary movement was being undercut by the division among the many Christian churches that were trying to evangelize. How does one explain to people who know nothing of splintered Christian history how a Methodist Christ differs from an Anglican Christ; why Catholics would not deal with Protestants; why, in the same name of Jesus, churches attacked each other?

Would it not make much more sense for one Christian church to announce one Christ to one world?

Through the Faith and Order movements in Europe in the early part of this century, to the growth of ecumenical efforts among Protestant churches, to the entrance of the Orthodox churches into religious dialogue, and finally to the acceptance by the Roman Catholic Church during the Second Vatican Council of the importance of ecumenism, churches have moved toward unity spurred, not by some self-destructive need to be wishy-washy, but by the evangelical imperative to be one, the one church that Jesus obviously willed, rather than the divided churches that so obviously contradict the message of Jesus.

Yet in spite of this profound historical connection, the populist images of ecumenism and evangelization have them living in worlds widely separated, speaking different accents, dialects and even languages. People can even wonder if ecumenism and evangelization can survive in the same Christianity.

Essential Connections

Less casual observation, however, brings out the realization that, instead of being rival children of the same gospel, evangelization and ecumenism have *essential* connections, links so basic that the one cannot really be conceived without the other.

What might some of these links be? Here are some of the obvious ones.

1) Evangelization and ecumenism share the same goal: that human-ity be joined in the unity of the kingdom of God.

Evangelization and ecumenism have the same ultimate vision. The ecumenical vision consists of the Christian family being one household, in unity and fellowship; at the same time, that house-hold fellowship should be "global"—world-wide. The term "ecu-menism" comes from the same root as our word for "econo-my"—the Greek word *oikos* which means literally "house" but fig-uratively connotes a "wide circle." In this wide—and ever wider!—circle, the ecumenical vision includes, first of all, all church com-munions that profess faith in Jesus Christ and, because of that belief, wish to grow in greater understanding.

If ecumenism begins with the minimal goal of increasing understanding, it goes on, through the faith that is the basis of ecumenical dialogue, to the maximum vision of people united in faith in the One God who draws all into unity. Perhaps the great-est challenge for Christian ecumenism and interfaith outreach will not revolve around intra-Christian discussion—as difficult as that is—but interreligious dialogue with other world religions. After all, Christians share the same New Testament images of the banqueters gathered into the kingdom, of the Lord gather-ing the nations, of Jesus praying that there be one flock and one Shepherd. Part of the agenda in the dialogue that must take place between Christians and other world religions has to involve this Christian vision and whether such dreams of unity make any sense at all to other world faiths. The gospel of Jesus, no matter who reads it, wants to be universal.

Evangelization has this same ultimate vision. Pope Paul VI, when he laid out the starting point of Catholic evangelization as that had been elaborated by a synod of bishops from around the world in 1974, began his reflections with the vision of humanity transformed. Evangelization dreams of a humanity renewed, changed, restored, healed and unified through the Good News of Jesus. Its vision also is global, universal and sweeping. From the coming of Jesus in our human flesh—with all that means for our humanity itself—to the gathering of a transformed people

presented to God by the Lord, evangelization pushes the edges
of our collective needs and hopes.

God invites us into God's household, God's family, God's
kingdom. Ecumenist and evangelist are, each of them, both
inviter and invited.

*2) Evangelization calls people to hear the Good News anew in their
personal and church lives; ecumenism likewise calls churches to hear
the Good News and respond in the Holy Spirit to the call for Christian
unity that Christ desired for his church.*

The Good News of Jesus lies at the basis of both evangelization and ecumenism. This message begins with a call to
"change"—the *metanoia* that asks for a change of mind, of out-
look, of imagination. Of course, the change calls people from
past lives of sin to new lives focused on God. But the call seems
more sweeping than this. More than our backgrounds of sin and
alienation, the Good News challenges the background of our
expectations about ourselves, our hopes and fears, what we conclude that life is all about, what we settle for in the limitation of
our human myopia. "Change! The kingdom of God is at hand!"

The change that Jesus invites us to sweeps across our personal
and collective lives. Paul VI, laying out further what evangelization means, refused to see it simply as a personal call to renewal.
The Good News of Jesus lays demands on our individual and
our collective consciences and involves a complex set of elements that go beyond personal response. (See *On Evangelization
in the Modern World,* nos. 18, 19 and 24.)

Yet, once we have heard Good News and, becoming disciples,
undertake a way of life based on that Good News in Christian
community, we have not finished our journey. Nor has our
Christian community finished its journey. For if individuals need
to continually hear God's Good News against the background of
the ever-changing demands of their lives so, too, must Christian
churches. *Ecclesia semper reformanda est* was the rallying cry
behind the Second Vatican Council: *the church must always be
reformed.*

The church and other ecclesial communions, hearing God's

word again and again, cannot be content to bow their heads and absolve themselves from all ecclesial implications of the proclaimed word of God. No ecclesial group has so listened to that word that it needs to listen no more. And, in principle, as long as churches experience disunity, they have not heard that word completely.

Conversion means individuals change; it also means that churches must change too.

3) Evangelization seeks the conversion of individuals and societies; ecumenism entails the conversion of church communities. Even as we profess that the fullness of Christ's church subsists in the Catholic Church, we acknowledge our own sinfulness and constant need to reform.

The ideals of evangelization and ecumenism have no chance of fulfillment unless church groups also accept the call to conversion, to acknowledge the limits of their own experiences and visions, and the invitation to grow beyond these through the call of Jesus into his kingdom. Even the Catholic Church, in which the Second Vatican Council taught us fullness of revelation subsists, still needs to experience greater, ongoing conversion to the gospel it proclaims, even as it has experienced profound conversion over these past thirty years.

The Catholic Church, for example, has experienced a profound change in the way it celebrates and lives under the word of God. Of course, the church has always lived by the holy scriptures. These sacred writings came from the experience of the church, its faithful reading and preserving them, its study and its proclamation of them over the centuries. But no one can doubt that, since Renaissance days, the church, in its public worship, proclaimed only a small portion of the scriptural texts. Before the reforms of the Second Vatican Council, the first reading came only from the letters of Paul, mumbled in Latin against the back wall of the church; the gospel reading invariably came from Matthew's gospel, mumbled in the same fashion. While Catholics knew of the Hebrew scriptures, and at times heard various "texts" from the prophets or the wisdom books, these writ-

ings were not a regular part of the public proclamation of the
church until the book of liturgical readings was reformed.

That reformation happened in part because of the witness
given to the word by other Christian ecclesial communities. The
veneration of the word by many Protestant groups formed the
background of this significant Catholic conversion.

Likewise, an elaboration of Catholic life almost totally in
terms of merit has given way to a more balanced presentation of
the Christian journey as grounded in the experience of grace.
Of course, Catholics have always believed that God's gracious
love is the foundation of Christian life. Nevertheless, the
renewed understanding of Catholics today owes a lot to the
accord given to the doctrine of grace by Protestants.

Both of these developments, we have to notice, have strong
roots in evangelization—the power of God's word and the fundamental message of grace which that word proclaims.

If the church must always be reformed, future contacts
between Catholics, Protestants and Orthodox will call for
future experiences of conversion, for every one of those
groups. Engaging in ecumenical dialogue means that churches
must be open to the direction of the Holy Spirit and to ongoing conversion.

*4) Both evangelization and ecumenism exclude proselytism and reli-
gious manipulation as a way to approach people. Each rests on the
assumption that God works mysteriously in the lives of other people and
that they are to be called with respect and dignity to hear the Good
News.*

Before churches adopted ecumenism as a basic framework,
religious life and talk was characterized by attacks and counter
attacks. Each church developed defenses around itself as it
lobbed accusations and generalizations toward other groups.
Dogmas were assembled, not to articulate the range of Christian
faith, but to buttress a church's historical or social situation and
to call into disrepute other churches' approaches.

At the same time, churches accompanied these attacks and
counterattacks with the presumption that members of other

groups were damned and that they had to be "converted" to "our church" in order to be saved.

While the problem of ecclesial divisions still looms over Christianity and while substantial differences between Christian communions still exist, Christian churches do not talk about "converting" members of other churches, as if members from another church were unevangelized or unbelievers! When baptized people join the Catholic Church, for example, their baptisms and faith experiences in other Christian churches are honored and respected.

Ecumenism has taught churches to talk with each other, to look each other in the eyes, to respect what is being said, to attend to each other's experiences. It has made clear that, unless the human person is respected, Christianity has no foundation.

Evangelization must, of course, rest on exactly the same assumption that, when we are proclaiming our faith to others, we truly attend to, respect and address those others in their human reality. Anything else is proselytism, manipulation, trickery and a disgrace to the good news that is supposedly being proclaimed.

Centuries of "rice Christian" approaches (in which missionaries got converts by giving freebies to native peoples), colonizing, patronizing and sometimes even grossly exploiting people, along with generations of "Elmer Gantry" experiences of evangelism (with all the attendant scandals) have obscured the fact that, in evangelization, believers address those called to belief with respect, honor and profound love. Without these, in fact, the gospel has no chance of really being heard. It is ecumenism which may teach us these fundamental human dynamics.

5) Evangelization recognizes that people of other churches and faiths may be invited to the fullness of the Catholic faith even as it acknowledges that God is working through these other churches and faiths. While no one will ever be turned away from seeking membership in the Catholic Church, neither will Catholics deny that God is using other churches as ways to call people to holiness.

Ecumenism is a way of evangelizing. Through ecumenism,

churches are being called to the church of Jesus Christ and the fullness of the gospel which Catholics believe subsists in their church. A delicate balancing act is needed, obviously, because while people are invited to this fullness of faith, this cannot mean that their particular faith and church experience is to be scorned or disparaged.

In other words, churches need both a short and a long term view. In the short term, people will be attracted to how Christian life is lived in different churches and, inevitably in a very mobile society, people will move from one church to another. This will be a cause both for grief and for joy; churches should recognize their own ambivalence about it. Should a Catholic, no longer practicing his or her faith, start living a Christian way of life as a Baptist or Presbyterian, Catholics will both rejoice that this person has begun following Christ and grieve that this following could not be done as a Catholic. Likewise, in the short term, churches must continue to grow in appreciation and dialogue of each other's expressions of faith; this will only happen through dramatically increased ecumenical contact.

In the long term, churches need to all look to the day when Christianity will have attained a unity, a world-wide community, when they will transcend the sectarianism and denominationalism (and the petty jealousies) that scar Christian experience. Only with that view kept before their eyes will Christians have the perspective to work through the ambiguities of our current Christian disarray with hope and patience.

6) Evangelization can help ecumenism celebrate diversity in unity.

What, after all, does "one church" mean? Often one gets the impression it means one totally unified and uniform experience of worship and spirituality. But this has never been the case in Christian life, as the gospels and scriptures themselves attest on the one hand and Christian history confirms on the other.

Evangelization, in the scriptural account itself, shows the tremendous diversity the proclamation of the gospel brings about. We can sense the differences in the early church between the communities at Corinth and Ephesus, as well as the emphases given the gospel by Luke's Greek and largely gentile community and Matthew's more Jewish one. Scriptural renewal has us reading John with a freshness that dramatically shows the more contemplative and symbolic forms of Christian life that marked Christian life in Asia Minor.

These experiences of diversity can provide a blueprint for ecumenical goals today: that a world-wide church communion does not mean a uniformity either of church organization nor of Christian spirituality. In fact, the diversity existing within the Catholic community, with its variety of rites, itself reveals the kind of plurality Christianity begets.

This plurality, explored through ecumenical sensitivity, can afford a newly united Christianity the opportunity for great witness as it seeks to address both global and modern needs, for people are not alike all over the world, and contemporary experience will continue to open up new challenges. The first evangelization, as experienced by the apostles through the book of Acts, offers a wide basis for hope.

Not by Words Alone

These considerations of the essential connections between evangelization and ecumenism mean nothing without continued experiences of church unity. When people don't have contact with other people, they start considering them as "different" and "strange," whether for racial, cultural or religious reasons. We cannot dismiss people whom we are talking to.

Ecumenism might be greatly helped by shared evangelization. This has already started to happen. Many Catholic dioceses, for example, have participated in evangelism crusades presented by the Billy Graham Crusade. In some areas, Catholics and Protestants have had joint revivals, renewals and "missions." There is widespread shared Bible study and discussion, although this frequently happens on a more informal level.

Evangelization, of course, is always calling people to a "table," to a particular community, because God does not invite us to some kind of religious abstraction like "Christianity" or

"Catholicism." Even so, without sending confusing messages by glossing over basic differences and pretending a unity that doesn't exist, Catholic, Protestant and Orthodox churches can share certain evangelizing activities with a lot of credibility. For example:

—Various churches can undertake a joint visitation of either a new housing development or an older development, seeking people who do not actively practice faith, and inviting them to different churches, based on their past affiliation. Each visitor can bring information about the "churches in our area" and be prepared to answer questions.

—Churches can cooperate, too, in efforts to encourage people to be more active in the practice of their faith. The world will not be worse off if most people worshipped regularly! Campaigns to stimulate involvement in church and church activities will help all the Christian communions.

—Various congregations can sponsor joint scripture discussion and study. Enough common translations exist and a sufficient awareness of exegetical methods is shared at least among mainline religious groups to make this quite possible. How the scriptures shed light on the practices of various Christian churches will more than reward such an effort.

—Churches can likewise agree on common courtesies that should attend evangelizing techniques and provide a forum for congregations that do not respect these common courtesies. Such an ecumenical framework for calling churches to evangelize with integrity can advance both the ecumenical and evangelizing goals of Christians today.

The Same Goal

The Holy Spirit has been calling Christian communions to great maturity through the ecumenical movement; in this century, this movement has dramatically reshaped the mentality of all Christian churches. It is quite possible that the Spirit is inviting the churches to an even newer level of maturity in which evangelization and ecumenism will not be seen as antagonists but as complementary forces, each with a special gift for highlighting the power of the gospel.

If ecumenism runs the risk of making religion look relativistic and if evangelization runs the risk of making churches arrogant, the mixing of these ministries, in a more sweeping vision, might save Christianity from two equally deadly vices. Christians without a message are a contradiction; Christians with arrogance are a failure. May the Spirit spare us from both.

10

Evangelization and Conversion

As Catholics begin to adopt a framework of evangelization, with its emphasis on Good News and biblical language, it will be most natural for them to employ concepts, strategies and mind-sets from Protestant, evangelistic patterns. Yet because of the differences between Catholic and evangelical theologies, some of these patterns should not be employed without great reflection and even a bit of caution. Two notions which one regularly hears about in evangelization are *conversion* and *kerygma*. This chapter offers a bit of reflection and caution about how these patterns might be adopted by Catholics.

"Converted men as a class are indistinguishable from natural men; some natural men even excel some converted men in their fruits...."[1] So wrote the famous American psychologist William James stating that, in effect, there is no difference between the converted and the unconverted. This remark, made toward the middle of his famous work, *Varieties of Religious Experience,* a study of conversion from the angle of Protestant evangelical religion, certainly is startling. Page after page, James gives vivid accounts of conversion, presenting the accounts of young people finally giving up drink or lust or other patterns of sin as they turn themselves over to Jesus and feel enormous peace. They have made a transition. They finally know life's meaning. They have been converted.

How, then, can James claim there is no difference between the converted and the unconverted?

---

1 William James, *Varieties of Religious Experience,* Lecture 10, "Conversion Concluded" (Collier, London, 1969), p. 195.

Our first response wants to reject James' claim. Of course there's a difference, we say. His book documents that difference. Every one of us has known people who have gone through tremendous changes in life—changes we can attribute only to faith or divine power. The word "conversion" itself implies change, turning around from one thing to another. So how can someone claim no difference between the converted and the unconverted?

Perhaps, we muse, James is talking statistically. Look at people who claim conversion as a whole, as a "class" to use James's phrase: are their lives different? Do not they have the same patterns of drinking, or cursing, or infidelity, or greed as everyone else? Conversion doesn't solve every problem or change every person completely. Maybe when we think about people who have experienced conversion as a "class," both before and long after conversion, James may have a point. As a whole, there may not be statistical differences; in the long run, all groups look the same.

In other words, there is the issue of "backsliding." Converted people, having reached some definitive juncture of their lives, finally surrendering or giving themselves over, still have not reached a true end or a final result. After the conversion, after the shift, some of the same old patterns can emerge again and, sliding back, one's behavior might look the same five years after conversion as it did before. For every converted person we know, do we not also know a formerly converted person? They were "born again," and confessed their faith in Jesus but, three years later, they left their wives or got involved in a robbery or just gave up religion.

Do not studies also show that people from some of the churches that most emphasize adult conversion, such as the Baptists, report proportionately the same as any other group, numbers of members who are no longer involved in that church? The Gallup Organization, studying people who have stopped going to many different kinds of churches, report "inactive" church members that roughly parallel the size of each church in the population. Large population churches, for example, have large numbers of people who stopped attending; smaller ones have smaller numbers of inactive people.[2]

The point, though, is that all churches, whatever their style of bringing people into faith, to Jesus, through conversion, have their "backsliders," their inactive members or their outright former members. So what can conversion mean if it can be so short-lived?

Even more than these statistical ideas, however, we have our own experience: how many times in our lives have we reached and crossed a juncture, a time for change, a time to finally lay things aside and, almost in surrender, give ourselves over to something else, to Someone else. Yet, one or two years later, we find ourselves in the same situation: reviewing our lives, trying to rid ourselves of things that must yet be eliminated, turning ourselves over to God once again because we know that, apart from God, surely no change will happen.

Yet, God or no God, does change really ever happen in life? We know that the cycle continues—Lent after Lent, retreat after retreat, crossroad after crossroad. Even when patterns of sin in our lives have been eliminated, other patterns start to show themselves.

So one way of putting James' observation into a question would be: does conversion ever really happen? And, even more, how does the raising of this question affect what we mean by the term "conversion"?

Ongoing Conversion

Some people have a pretty clear picture of conversion. They present it quite simply.

I have a little pamphlet, not bigger than three by four inches, filled with cartoons. The cartoons depict the process of conversion. The message is presented around the first letters of the word "graced." God loves us; rebellion from humans breaks this

---

[2] The Gallup Organization, *The Unchurched American* (PNCEA, Washington, DC, 1988), p. 54.

love; the answer is Jesus; choose Jesus in your heart; eternal life begins when we say "Yes" to Jesus; depend on Jesus for your spiritual growth. Although we cannot save ourselves, we can *choose* to be saved by God in Jesus. Conversion is as simple as that.[3]

This cartoon schema does not differ greatly from the famous four-point process of conversion. Many people look at these points as the "ladder" or "skeleton structure" of faith; one proceeds up those points to an inevitable final point, a point of conversion. The points go something like this:

- The first point is God's creation and Adam's sin. Here are Adam and Eve, happy in the Garden of Eden and a few frames later, here they are naked and ashamed outside the Garden, locked out forever.
- The second point is God's justice, demanding some kind of tit-for-tat response for this sin. But who can respond justly to God? How can infinite justice be satisfied?
- Which leads to the third point: God, knowing that his infinite justice could not be satisfied by merely finite people, sends the Son, Jesus, to suffer in our place and satisfy God's justice. Jesus purchases, if you will, all that humans need from God.
- Lastly, the justice of Jesus is open to everyone who accepts him in his or her heart. Doing this brings assurance of salvation, of friendship from God and life eternal in heaven. It may also, as an extra dividend, bring great satisfaction in life (and, some might even claim, financial security).

There's the ladder, the simple steps ready to be scaled, until the point of faith, the acceptance of Jesus in our hearts.

Showing how simple the process of conversion reputedly is, however, does not eliminate the problem of backsliding. What if I ascend the ladder and go through all the points and accept Jesus in my heart, but then I sin, seriously and gravely, again?

There are two answers that, variously, are given to this prob-

---

[3] Good Shepherd Community, Inc. (Orlando, FL).

lem. One simply says that one must repent and, in effect, be converted again. The other says that, though one may sin or one may seem to sin, the grace of God cannot be doubted and the assurance of salvation cannot be taken away. God asks me to change, for sure, but I am, in spite even of my sin, still justified—a position quite close to Martin Luther, who saw Christians as simultaneously sinners and justified.

In the one version, conversion leads to successive conversions, perhaps, but it is not a definitive ending point. In the other version, conversion seems quite definitive, but one cannot verify that entirely in terms of behavior. In either version, after conversion one sins again, one backslides. So maybe conversion doesn't happen as a "once and for all" sort of thing, whatever people claim. There may not be, simply speaking, conversion, but only ongoing conversion.

Kerygma and Conversion

The four steps of our ladder, which were to lead us to conversion, are a kind of shorthand for what is called "kerygma." This Greek word means "message"—it derives from the image of an announcement made after a horn (*keryx*, in Greek) is blown to get attention. "Kerygma" refers to the "heart" of the Christian message. "Kerygma" should stir and shake us; it should make us not only attend to the message, but want to do something about it. It should make us likely to respond "yes" as we get to the climactic point of decision: now that you have heard this message, what will you do about it?

Certain evangelical techniques, somewhat following the four-step ladder we saw above, move people to this critical question. For example, in *Evangelism Explosion*, Dr. Kennedy asks would-be home visitors to learn certain passages from the scriptures; some of these passages come from the Old Testament, particularly the book of Genesis and the Prophets, while others come from the New Testament. They set up the same dilemma as our book of cartoons or the "ladder" of salvation: we've sinned, we can do nothing, and what will we do about it? When it becomes clear that one can attain salvation only by accepting Jesus, the home visitors are taught to propose this question: "Do you want to receive this gift of eternal life that Christ left heaven and died on the cross to give you?"[4] A positive response leads to salvation. This method has been employed not only by evangelical Protestants but also by some Roman Catholic groups.

Yet is this the kerygma? Is kerygma so simple and so stark? Christians must ask where this cartoon kerygma, or the four-step kerygma, or Dr. Kennedy's visiting routine comes from? Where does any "kerygma" come from? And why have so few people heard it? One may respond that the kerygma comes from the Bible, of course. But does it really? If Dr. Kennedy and many other evangelicals can presume that most mainline churches have members who have not been evangelized in them, where does his understanding of the "essential message" come from? What *are* these churches doing when they read the very same scriptures?

Can it be that evangelicals are calling for a certain *pattern of response* that they believe constitutes evangelization and have developed a "formula" from certain scriptures that they believe lead one to the pattern that they stipulate is required for salvation? On what is this pattern based? Are we warranted to shrink the kerygma down to a succinct formula, a direct plea and a close-to-inevitable answer?

Certain Catholic renewal movements likewise focus in on kerygma. The point of these movements is to give Catholics a particular *experience* of salvation. In this case, the kerygma serves as more than a "message"; it is also as vehicle for this experience. Not only does the kerygma present the message of the sheer grace of God (saving us in spite of our sin and apart from any deed or merit on our part) but it also wants to present the counterpart to this kerygma, the experience of *unconditional love.* In this case, the kerygma demands a response; salvation is the acceptance of unconditional love (and feeling of unconditional

---

[4] Dr. D. James Kennedy, *Evangelism Explosion: The Coral Ridge Program for Lay Witness* (Tyndale, Wheatin, IL, 1970-1983), pp. 17–23.

love). Insofar as mainline Christians may not have *experienced* this unconditional love, they have not heard the kerygma, and have not been converted or evangelized. So the argument would run.

What is the feeling of unconditional love? Or, in its theological dress, what is the experience of "grace"—which seems to many people to be equivalent to unconditional love? When we realize that, before anything and in spite of everything, we are loved, we have experienced unconditional love. The kerygmatic form would put it: God loves us unconditionally (and he sent Jesus to prove it). Realizing that we are loved before everything and in spite of anything can take many forms, the most prominent one today coming in an "I'm OK, You're OK" format. Are the scriptures requiring a particular form of believers?

To get closer to our understanding of what conversion is, we need to look more closely at kerygma and see whether the scriptural tradition can be defined by something like a four-step kerygma and a correlative feeling attached to an experience of unconditional love.

Kerygmas and Kerygma

Jesus begins his preaching, at least in several of the gospels, with virtually the same message as John the Baptist. "Repent, the kingdom of God is near."

While we all know what the word "repent" means, at the same time we all have the word somewhat askew. For years, the word "repent" was understood as "do penance," the kinds of deeds that Catholics undertake during Lent: fasting, denying oneself of pleasures, giving alms and performing extra deeds of loving service. The very readings at the start of Lent, however, give another shade to this word by urging Catholics not to undertake these as external performances but as the means of interior change.

So we can also understand "repent," for instance, as "give up your sin," and, in this way, it does mean more than "do penance," because it asks us to draw a line between how we were "before" and how we want to be "after." Certainly, most believers realize that conversion means the giving up of sin. Catholics, who start Lent "doing penance," end Lent on Easter Sunday morning by rejecting Satan and the forces of evil, as they profess their faith in the Triune God.

But if "repent" means that we give up sin, it still can mean something else too. The root meaning of repent, in Greek, comes close to this: "change your mind around." Change your attitude. Change the way you see things. In this sense, the command of Jesus is not only about sin, nor need it be primarily articulated in terms of sin. It is articulated in terms of one's whole being. Jesus is asking us to look toward an alternate future, different from any past (hence, "change"); this gives us access to the incoming kingdom he proclaims.

When Jesus said these things, what was he asking? Did he assume, as some scholars argue, that the world would quickly end and was he calling for decisive action in view of that impending calamity? Was he asking people to join a movement, a church, an experiment? After his death and resurrection, was the message of his disciples different from his? It seems that kerygma, rather than being a straightforward simple formula, is laden with layers of meanings and questions.

Kerygma and Personal Experience

The scriptures clearly show a distinct relationship between the message and the hearing, between the kerygma and the person who responds to it. In fact, when we look at the gospel accounts we find a great variety of ways that people experienced and responded to Jesus. Evangelization, as the receiving of the "message," took on many forms in Christ's ministry in response to both his deeds and his words.

Very often, the Lord addressed people by driving out demons; evangelization, therefore, meant some kind of liberation from possession. Quite frequently, too, Jesus addressed people by bringing healing and salvation, which meant being made whole. We frequently see Jesus teaching the crowds or his disciples, showing that evangelization meant discipleship, the capacity to hear, be influenced by, and follow Jesus. On a few occasions, the presence of Jesus brings about a return from the dead. Sometimes, too, evangelization means the forgiveness of sin— once, quite explicitly, with the curing of the paralyzed man (Mark 2:1-10). Each of these evangelizing moments is "kerygma," the drawing near of God in Christ Jesus. In each case there is a "response," whether it be liberation, healing, discipleship, forgiveness or even resurrection. In many of these cases, the response does not depend entirely on the person being addressed.

Even after people are gathering into the church we see great variations in the response to the kerygma. After conversion, there is yet a tremendous acknowledgment of ongoing sin and imperfection. The first letter to the Corinthians deals, chapter by chapter, with the moral, doctrinal and communal limitations of that community. Parables about weeds growing up alongside wheat (Matthew 13:24-30) and about the invited guests (Matthew 22:1-14) certainly acknowledge that the early church contained both "good" and "bad" people; as the latter parable puts it, "The servants. . . rounded up everyone, the bad as well as the good." Stories such as the lost sheep, the lost coin and the lost son (i.e., the prodigal son) likewise highlight the openness of the early Christians to sinners, presumably even those in their midst (Luke 15:1-31). Even passages that depict an ideal Christian community, such as at the end of Acts 4:42, get followed almost immediately by less ideal stories, such as the report of the cheating and death of Ananias and Sapphira in the very next chapter (Acts 5:1-11). Surely the sins and failures are not held up as ideals (quite the contrary), but neither is the picture one of unbroken perfection.

In other words, a fuller reading of the scriptural texts shows, in the message of Jesus and the resulting response, a tremendous variation. People heard it differently according to the actual needs of their own lives; and the result was not instantaneous change or miraculous transformation, but the beginning of a journey that would entail ongoing struggle, insight and growth.

In terms of the Christian message, how should the kerygma

be proposed to people today? Are the formulas we saw above, the four-step ladder or the one built upon the word "graced" the only way the New Testament presents Jesus? Can contracting the kerygma into simple formulas and clear propositions do justice to what we see happening in the New Testament itself, the great variation of call, response and subsequent growth?

A Counter-Kerygma

In fact, when we try to look at the way many of these simplified kerygmas hang together, they might inadvertently obscure the very God they seek to manifest. In almost every instance, these formulas of the kerygma have the death of Jesus somehow appeasing a God whose justice demands some divine vengeance, whose wrath is ready to be spilled over on those who do not respond. God has loved us unconditionally, he had Jesus die to prove it, he asks us to believe in this Jesus or else be damned forever. Is this the picture of God that Jesus himself cultivated and that the New Testament primarily supports? We need to explore this a bit in wider biblical terms.

The book of Deuteronomy, in the Old Testament, had a line of thinking that influenced almost all the composition of the Bible: if we are faithful to God, God will be faithful to us, care for us and make us prosper. "Do what is right in the sight of the Lord, that you may, according to his word, prosper, and may enter into and possess the good land which the Lord promises on oath to your fathers, thrusting all your enemies out of your way" (Deuteronomy 6:18–19). But the opposite is also proposed: "If, however, you turn away your hearts and will not listen, but are led astray and adore and serve other gods, I tell you now that you will certainly perish; you will not have a long life on the land which you are crossing the Jordan to enter and occupy" (Deuteronomy 30:17–18).

This Deuteronomic view, however, is questioned in the Old Testament writings in the book of Job and in parts of the book of Ecclesiastes. Job gives us the image of a perfectly just person who nonetheless suffers the loss of everything important to him;

Ecclesiastes sees life as an endless cycle rather than an exchange
of fidelities. "There is nothing new under the sun; all is vanity,"
the book says (see Ecclesiastes 1:2,9). On top of these, the scriptures narrate the tragic exile of the Jews into captivity, which, in
addition to acknowledging the sin of God's people also raises
questions about God's own faithfulness (see Psalm 44 and
Lamentations 2). In other words, it may not be a simple tit-for-
tat proposition.

At their deepest level of meaning, the Christian scriptures
shake this Deuteronomic vision to its foundation because they
narrate how Jesus, the innocent one, is condemned as a sinner
and dies in shame and abandonment. Contradicting the vision
of Deuteronomy and expanding the complaint of Job, Jesus, in
his innocence, suffers an utterly shameful death. Long life and
prosperity do not invariably accompany goodness; there is no
simple connection between success and goodness, failure and
sin (see John 9:2). The Christian vision pushes beyond that of
the Deuteronomic tradition.

This means that "justice" cannot contract down to a simple
"tit-for-tat" picture—do good and God will take care of you; do
evil and God will condemn you. Rather than showing the inex-
orable justice of God, the New Testament shows the surprising
grace of God, a grace revealed in raising Jesus from the dead
and offering salvation and mercy to everyone, Jew and non-Jew
alike. It is not simply the grace of "unconditional love," but the
upsetting of the usual categories we use to think about God and
ourselves. Rather than the wrath of God driving the logic of the
New Testament, God's mercy dominates.

In other words, we have to seriously question whether the
threat of God is the primary driving force of the New Testament
message and whether one's response to the New Testament
should primarily be one of repentance from sin because of the
impending wrath of God. Is not the message broader and the
pattern of response more varied?

I am not arguing that God does not demand holiness, fidelity,
commitment and the rejection of sin. There are words of threat
in the gospels and the letters of St. Paul, as well as the book of

Revelation. Paul sees Jesus' death as saving us from the wrath of God (Romans 5:8–9) and even talks about God handing over Jesus as an offering (Romans 3:25 and Ephesians 5:2).

Yet, surely, a God whom Christians believe so readily forgives cannot be the blood-thirsty God who will not save people unless his beloved Son dies shamelessly on the cross. It makes little sense to paint God in monster colors in order to explain why Jesus died or why people should experience conversion. The more savage God appears, the less people will be attracted.

So how *can* the death of Jesus be seen? Apart from the idea of appeasing God's wrath, it can also be understood as a generous giving, both on the side of Jesus who so obeys his calling that he accepts the death that goes along with it, and on the side of God who, in Jesus, demonstrates his complete love for us. Instead of the death of Jesus being a function of God's justice, it might more cogently be a function of God's total love and self-revelation in Jesus, "up to the end," as John's gospel puts it (John 13:1), including death. The death of Jesus occurs, not because of some legal schemata of justice, but because of the logic of God's entering a sinful world and dealing with our human condition completely, including death.

A contracted kerygma can become a "counter-kerygma" in which people, upon hearing it, are invited to respond to a rather vicious God who needed Jesus' blood in order to be satisfied— and who may need our own as well! Rather than freeing people up to respond to a God whose love invites and involves them in the actual dilemmas of their lives, it can be a box that manipulates people into patterned responses to a canned message.

Kerygma and Conversion

If the kerygma is about God's total love for us in the offering made to us in Jesus Christ, who assumes our natures and even our death to bring us a new view of God and a new relationship with God, then what would the experience of salvation, of hearing that message, look like? I propose the following. *The experience of conversion is a turning to God in complete fidelity as Jesus*

showed in his life and death. It is not merely feeling God's unconditional love but involvement in the mystery of passing over
from oneself to God in the pattern of Christ Jesus.

One sees in the New Testament little of the "emotional"
instances of salvation that many modern evangelists seem to
insist are the "essence" of salvation—accepting Jesus as one's
"personal Lord and Savior." Certainly, in the New Testament we
see people rejecting their sins and turning to God, but this may
happen with or without a great consciousness. People accept
baptism in response to the word (e.g., Acts 2:41) and some communities in the New Testament enjoy charismatic gifts (see 1
Corinthians 12:1 ff.), but the gospel of Matthew shows a judgment scene in which the saved do not even know the good
deeds they did (Matthew 25:31 ff.). In one place we even see a
direct attack on the idea that professing "Lord" and doing miracles is a true following of Jesus (Matthew 7:21–24). Jesus shrewd-
ly gives us the image of the two sons, one enthusiastically saying
"Yes" but doing nothing, and the other rebelliously saying "No,"
but following God's will (Matthew 21:28–31). "Accepting Jesus"
in the New Testament means, more than anything, becoming his
disciple and being faithful for the long haul.

There is little preoccupation with the "assurance of salvation"
that modern evangelicals see as the hallmark of an evangelized
person. There is little involvement with breakthroughs of personal consciousness that people associate with conversion.
When Paul, for example, talks about believing in our hearts that
Jesus is Lord and confessing that with our lips (Romans 10:9), he
is hardly talking about our modern constructions of "Jesus consciousness." When we read these verses in their context, we
understand them as part of an elaborate treatment of God's
plan of salvation as it relates to Jews and non-Jews. Paul is
advancing his argument that non-Jews are also called by pointing
to the reality of non-Jewish religious experience in the church.
The actions of professing and believing, which take place in the
midst of a believing people, "lead to" salvation because they
involve us in discipleship, in ongoing discipleship.

The bishops of the United States saw evangelization as a

process of "making disciples" when they issued *Go and Make Disciples: A National Plan and Strategy for Catholic Evangelization in the United States.* Disciples, involved in church community, in prayer, sacrament, God's word and service, experience ongoing conversion which is authenticated by their relationships with others. Acknowledging conversion as the "change of our lives that comes about through the power of the Holy Spirit," they proceed to elaborate some of the many forms by which people undergo conversion, from sudden life changes, to family life, to religious education, to involvement in renewal movements.

Many modern constructions of kerygma, especially in their more extreme evangelical dress, are only abstractions and reconstructions of certain passages from the New Testament. In the end, they lead to their inevitable contradictions. If, after all, God's grace alone saves me, then why do I have to respond at all? If a response is all God wants, then why does it have to be accompanied by any feelings or behaviors? If God is so loving and forgiving, why will his anger lead to the eternal damnation of most human beings? If God "enlightens everyone born into the world," why do we assume everyone is so corrupt?

If our image of kerygma can be broader, our ideas about conversion might be more inclusive and truer to what God actually is asking of us.

Conversion: Turning to God

Let's return to the initial preaching of Jesus as Matthew and Mark portray it for us. "Turn your minds around," begins the preaching of Jesus; God's kingdom is near and, should we hesitate, we might miss it. If "repent" is asking us to turn away from our sins, it is primarily asking us to turn toward God. For all that God asks us to turn away from, most of all God asks us to turn toward that kingdom which, fundamentally, is God's own self.

How varied are the ways we can turn to and discover God! Some of us will turn toward that kingdom seeking joy and peace. Others will turn toward that kingdom seeking justice. Some will be wrapped in God's kingdom through the pursuit of truth.

Others will find God, and turn themselves over to God, through beauty. Many will seek God out of a desire for wholeness and healing. Only some of us will also be driven to God primarily by our shame and sinfulness.

But is it not absolutely clear that not everyone will begin to hear the message of the kingdom by being conscious of sin? Nor will everyone appropriate the kingdom through a sense of brokenness. Nor will a need to *feel* "unconditional love" be a necessary path for most. The more we make sin, brokenness and depravity the basis of hearing the message of Jesus and responding, the more we have to induce awareness of these in people who have already, in their lives, many other avenues into the kingdom of God. Shall we become doctors who must first make people feel sick before they come to our ministrations? Or shall we take people as God touches them?

When images of kerygma and what "evangelism" means begin to exclude most of the people who have heard, reflected on and tried to live the gospel, we should be suspicious and cautious. Further, when constructions of the kerygma distort our approach to people ("we have to convict them of sin") and hide the ways God is already involved in their lives, we should wonder whose needs are being served. When techniques seek to bring people to emotional and psychological breakthroughs that fit into preconceived categories of conversion rather than letting the breath of the New Testament and lived Christian experience speak to us, we may well have grounds to question these assumptions.

The central mystery of Christianity, the death and resurrection of Jesus, will become a form in the lives of people in many different ways in a life. After their entry into the church, Christians will continuously experience this death and resurrection, morally, spiritually, intellectually and vocationally. In this experience, they undergo a constant turning toward God, a turning around of the way they think and live as they face the future God invites them to.

Christians have called this the paschal mystery and, through prayer, sacrament and daily life, God has shaped their lives into the form of this mystery. Christians, in community, by celebrating the dying and rising of Christ, particularly in the sacraments and holy eucharist, are themselves formed in this pattern of Christ. While no one can enter the reality of Christ without this paschal experience, we are involved in this experience in many moments, at many times, in many forms in our lives.

Rather than a neat kerygma and a formula response, the paschal mystery, which invites us into the depths of God, also opens up the vastness of the presence of God's grace in human history and the continual power of ongoing conversion in the life story of every believer. Our conversion, our turning to God, will be formed by the way Christ's pattern of dying and rising is incorporated, in an ongoing way, into our Christian life.

Evangelization is the ministry that attends to the reality of conversion in Christian life. Starting with the proclamation of God's word in our human experience, it takes hold of our lives by relating them to the God of Jesus and to others as a way of life both personal and communal. It inserts our experience into the pattern of God's revelation, of Christ's dying and rising, and the emergence of God's kingdom in its fullness.

The kerygma is not a formulaic message but a drama as broad as humanity and as vast as God's wondrous kingdom.

11

The Sacramental Basis
of Catholic Evangelization

"On Sunday night," she was fiercely saying to me, "my brother will receive the Holy Spirit."

She was speaking about her brother, then about 15 years old, who had been deeply involved in the parish as an altar server, religious education student and youth group member for several years.

"How do you know he hasn't already received the Holy Spirit?" I answered just as fiercely.

Less than a year before, he had completed preparation to receive the sacrament of confirmation. He had worshipped regularly and consistently, had understood as much of Catholic teaching as 14-year-olds understand, participated on youth retreats and belonged to a very tight network of youth who had rejected the neighborhood's tendency toward drugs and sex and supported each other, through the parish and their friendships, in an alternative way of life.

But now this young man was going to leave our parish, our church and most of his neighborhood friends so that he could be "baptized again" and receive the Holy Spirit in a small Pentecostal church in which his sister was active. Had nothing been happening to him the years he was active in the parish? How did he come to get the notion that something *else* yet had to happen to him? Did the body and blood of Christ pale in comparison to people speaking ecstatically or the daily impression of miracles liberally given? Did the sacraments which play so powerful a role in the Catholic Church simply cease to play a role in his life? Or, perhaps, he simply never got the point of what God was already doing in his life.

"How do you know that he did not already receive the Holy Spirit?"

Sacraments

From my Catholic eyes, this young man and millions of others received the Holy Spirit at baptism because the Spirit comes as grace even to those who have not the consciousness to know it, and because the Spirit moves as the Spirit wants (cf. John 3:8). From my Catholic viewpoint, the Holy Spirit needs no extraordinary consciousness nor even an ordinary awareness to work in our hearts. The Holy Spirit, which is Jesus' greatest Easter gift, comes from the abundant outpouring of Christ's love upon all the faithful. The only sign my Catholic temperament asks is the sign of the Christian community rooted in God's word, in service and in the life of sacraments (I do not deny, of course, that the Holy Spirit can also come upon people who have not yet received the sacraments—the Spirit moves as it wants!).

To some non-Catholic Christians (and even to certain groups of Catholics) the Holy Spirit does not work so subtly. Perhaps Catholics receive the *promise* of the Holy Spirit at baptism, some might put it; a more negative assessment is that Catholics are only doing empty forms when they baptize children and going through empty ritual with the formulas of the mass. Many of these non-Catholics believe they know the Holy Spirit is present because of signs more dramatic than the pouring of water and the anointing with oil. When the tongue utters unknown languages or at least strange sounds of joy, when people are healed or when prophecies are received, when people can give a cogent and fervent account of their conversions or change of life, then they know the Holy Spirit is present.

So what has a sacrament done, if anything?

In fact, in subtle ways, all renewal movements can seem to question the evangelizing power of the sacraments. Even those movements that are not based on special experiences of the

Holy Spirit still insinuate that receiving a sacrament does not do much for a person; something more is needed—some experience, some change, some observable development beyond the receiving of baptism, confirmation and the frequent reception of holy communion. Even while these renewal movements reverence the sacraments and the sacramental way of life, they imply, in themselves, that the sacraments are not adequate in themselves. Something *else* is needed.

The paradoxical upshot of all this is that, from the viewpoint of renewal movements, the average, worshipping Catholic is not really evangelized. Sure, they come to church, they put in their envelopes, they send their children to Catholic school or religious education; but they haven't the spark, the enthusiasm, the fervor that renewal movements postulate. They haven't had the requisite experience to be truly evangelized.

The consequent implications of this attitude for evangelizing activity are enormous. Because if evangelization has to be directed at the average person in the pew (assuming such a creature actually exists), then the energy of evangelization will inevitably stay inward, focused on the gathered assembly, on the "average Catholic," on the ones "in the back of the church," rather than being an energy that reaches beyond the gathered assembly, inviting and involving those who have no church family or those who do not practice their faith. Furthermore, evangelization, from the point of view of these movements, will not consist of bringing people to the church, but involving people in the particular religious renewal movement that one judges as "evangelizing."

Sacramental Basis

When one surveys the classic approaches to evangelization sketched by Pope Paul VI and Pope John Paul II, it seems pretty clear that their view of evangelization hinges on the involvement of the person in the church through the sacraments. True, Christian life does not merely consist of receiving sacraments; it demands that we live differently and show those differences in the way we treat others. Yet the power to do just that—the direction, the meaning, the commandment, the energy and the Spirit—comes from being baptized into Christ and being sustained through the eucharist of Christ. Likewise, the sacraments of marriage and holy orders bring about a deeper following of the Lord in discipleship through particular ways of life. In reconciliation and through anointing, the power of Christ acts to make a person whole spiritually and physically.

We Catholics believe that Christ touches the lives of people in a particular way through the sacraments. Christ is the one who heals, forgives, joins, appoints, gives himself and saves. These movements crystallize the gospel's meaning as they make clear that God has come so close to us as to touch us through signs and symbols. They continue in contemporary life what Christ did in his own ministry, the touching and healing, the gathering at table, the calling and choosing. Again, to be fair to the Catholic position, we have to note that God can and does work at moments apart from sacramental ones, and that the sacraments themselves point to the action of God in the ordinary life of the Catholic beyond the ritual itself. Reconciliation, for example, points to the healing that has already taken place and has to continue to take place in someone's life, showing itself in the changed relationships someone has with others as well as a changed relationship with God. Acknowledging all of this, however, Catholic and papal thought has articulated evangelization primarily in terms of the church and its sacraments.

Can anything make this clearer than the Rite of Christian Initiation of Adults, the normal way adults enter the Catholic Church? The initial evangelization, the maturing inquiry, the continued journey through the catechumenate, the stage of enlightenment all lead to the reception of the sacraments of initiation. The mystagogia—the period after receiving the sacraments of initiation—continues to focus on the ongoing sacramental life of the newly initiated, although certainly not exclusively on that.

In fact, if one were to try to summarize the renewal of the Catholic Church begun at the Second Vatican Council, it could largely be done by saying that the church has tried to plumb its

sacramental reality and make that more efficacious in the daily
life of the Catholic. If once sacraments were rarely received and
barely understood, the reform of the church has looked for
sacraments to be frequently received and more deeply understood. If sacraments tended toward mere formality, modern
church reformers have pointed out how these sacraments were
primarily encounters with the living Christ, demanding the
change and renewal in life that Christ communicates through
the sacrament.

From this point of view, a Catholic could claim that an evangelized person is one who lives out the implications of his or her
sacramental life. In other words, *nothing else is asked* by Christ
than that his followers let the evangelizing power of the sacraments take hold of them and change their lives. The sacraments
bring salvation and continue to show salvation's presence in our
lives.

Conversion

Catholics do not easily talk "conversion" language. In chapter
10 we saw many reasons why that was so, principally stemming
from all the human and spiritual complexities that the idea of
conversion entails. Conversion, so often articulated in terms of
adults making personal decisions about accepting Jesus in
response to the scriptures, simply has to mean more for
Catholics whose theology runs more deeply than the "decision
of adults" and the "sufficiency" of God's word.

With a simple shift of language, however, Catholics can feel
quite at home with the notion of conversion understood as participation in the paschal mystery. Instead of accepting Jesus in
one's heart, Catholics speak more readily of dying and rising
with Christ. In Jesus, life comes through death, for the pivotal
moment in all existence is the self-giving of the Son totally on
the cross and the ratification of the Son's self-gift in the resurrection from the dead. That moment compresses the drama of all
human reality as ultimate human limits (sin, death) are tran-
scended through the action of God in Jesus Christ.

Since the earliest Christian writings, the sacraments have been understood as participation in this pivotal moment, in the paschal mystery. When Paul argues with the Corinthian community about the meaning of their worship, he points to the overwhelming realization that their eating and drinking are shares in the Lord's own death. As Catholics say at mass, directly following Paul's thought, "When we eat this bread and drink this cup, we proclaim your death Lord Jesus, until you come in glory" (see 1 Corinthians 11:23–26). For the "bread that we break, is it not a participation in the body of Christ?" In other words, the experience of the sacraments is an experience of being inserted into the reality of Christ Jesus, into his dying and rising.

Paul expresses the same notion when he talks about baptism to the Christian community at Rome. Were they aware that when they were baptized, they were baptized into Christ's death? "We were indeed buried with him through baptism into death, so that, just as Christ was raised from the dead by the glory of the Father, we too might live in newness of life" (Romans 6:4). Paul expands upon the "newness of life" that this sacramental participation brings about, for Christ's death entails our dying to sin so that we might live forever. Paul continues: "Therefore, sin must not reign over your mortal bodies . . . present yourselves to God as raised from the dead to life" (Romans 6:13).

Quite clearly, the paschal mystery is not restricted to some mystical moment in the past; the paschal mystery, the dying and rising of Christ, continues in the lives of Christ's followers as they undergo the experience of dying and rising in many forms in their daily lives. Such a notion is not that far removed from the words of Jesus that Matthew records to the effect that we must daily take up our crosses and follow Christ (Matthew 16:24–25).

If conversion can be understood as sharing in the paschal mystery, and if that sharing takes place in daily life, then conversion continues to happen as Christians are invited to deeper life through the many ways that death is experienced. For example, couples who marry through the sacrament of matrimony do so "in the Lord." Marriage is a sacrament precisely because it reflects the paschal mystery of Jesus, how Christ loved the church and gave himself for it (cf. Ephesians 5:25). Yet the dying and rising that marriage entails extends beyond having to leave one's own family to become "one flesh" with one's spouse. When the new household is formed, each party must continue to give, laying aside oneself for the sake of the other spouse. As the marriage matures, furthermore, relationships have also to mature, passing beyond simple romance and erotic attraction to profound bonding and belonging. (Perhaps so many break-downs in marriage, and so much infidelity, is exactly the refusal to live the paschal mystery in marriage.) Each of these moments in married life is a dying and rising, and each calls the married person to a deeper conversion, a deeper share in the paschal mystery of Christ.

If the sacraments bring about this participation in the paschal mystery of Christ, then obviously they are the experiences of conversion and concretize the many ways dying and rising takes place throughout all Christian life in its most profound events. Reflect on the dying and rising that ministry demands of those ordained, or the dying and rising that healing involves. Can someone be reconciled and experience forgiveness without dying enough to extend forgiveness to others? The sacraments point to the whole range of Christian experience which they cel-ebrate and concretize.

This, then, is the sacramental basis of Catholic evangelization: that if we truly receive the sacraments, if we truly live them and let them ground our lives, we will, because of our participation in Christ Jesus himself, undergo the constant conversion of dying and rising with him.

Sacramental Adequacy

With this kind of theological understanding of the sacra-ments, is it any wonder that the sacraments seem quite complete as evangelizing events in the lives of Catholics? What *else* can be needed than to share in the death and resurrection of Jesus

Christ and make the pattern of his paschal mystery the pattern of one's own life?

As the sacraments are received over time, the richness of their evangelizing nature stands out even more clearly because they become part of the rhythm of Catholic life. The moments consecrated by the sacraments become the focal moments of a person's, a family's and a community's existence. Parents promise, through the baptism of their infants, to raise their children as believers and make the faith the pattern of their lives. As children grow in their Christian initiation, the sacraments of confirmation and eucharist underline that growth. The weekly and frequent celebration of the eucharist engenders a pattern of life that pervades the work-week, as believers not only bring their concerns to the community's prayer, but also bring the community's worship to their newly begun week. Even the crisis moments of sickness and death come to be part of the profound rhythm of Catholic life.

Because of their human and earthly form, the sacraments have the power to insinuate themselves into the lives and consciousness of believers. Subtly, powerfully, they come to take hold of the way people live, the way family interact, the way nations understand themselves, the way cultures express their values.

If someone discovers Christ and gives up sin, is that inherently a better pattern than if someone, through Christian education and formation, is able to evade that sin in the first place? If a person has his or her mind opened for the first time through the reading of scriptures, is that superior to that person being formed by the scriptures from birth? Does a sudden, shattering conversion seem more attuned to actual human life, or is the daily dying to self and living for God not closer to the way we actually live and grow?

The sacraments, so easily put down as empty forms and papal foppery, actually correspond to the communal and cultural patterns that lie at the heart of our human experience. The sacraments challenge and transform us personally and culturally. They shape individual and collective lives. They insert God into human experience. The very formality of the sacraments, the gestures, rituals and material forms, nudge the believer into patterns of faith that come to take life over. On any particular day, a believer may not be disposed to fervent prayer and deep contemplation; during times in someone's life, faith may seem more lively or more quiet; but over the long haul, the sacraments tie people and communities, whatever is happening at a particular moment, into the paschal mystery of Jesus Christ. They wrap themselves around our humanity and thus make faith as palpable as human existence itself.

Two Languages

The current world of Catholic evangelization tends to use the same set of words, but behind the uniform vocabulary there may well be two very different languages coming from two different views of faith. Everyone talks renewal, God's word, Christ-at-the center, Holy Spirit, workplace spirituality, witness and discipleship. But Catholics who come from a sacramental point of view understand these as flowing from the kind of dynamic spirituality they associate with worship which is the heart of evangelization. Catholics whose perspective is not sacramental, who perhaps come from one or another renewal movement (especially those who have somewhat evangelical and Pentecostal routes) see these at the heart of evangelization, with the sacraments supplying the role of *helping* evangelization along.

One framework sees the church as a natural context for evangelization since the sacraments are at the heart (though not exclusively) of the life of the church. Worship, especially in eucharist, forms the center of evangelization. The other framework sees evangelization primarily as an inner, personal consciousness; it can almost do without church, although some kind of community usually always accompanies renewal experiences—the community of the "enlightened" or of those who have passed through the same special experience. One framework relates the believer to the world, because church in its fullest form engages the world; the other often helps the believer escape from a world judged evil. In the mentality of one frame-work, church is the ultimate achievement; in the language of the other, church is the minimum starting point.

Look, for example, at Latin American forms of Christianity. Until recently, these were primarily Catholic and expressed in terms of the church and its sacraments. For all the folk and fami-ly forms of religion that have developed throughout the range of nations influenced by Iberian Catholicism (perhaps in large mea-sure because of the absence of sufficient clergy to provide the sacraments), still the celebration of sacramental rites have been the principal organizing points of these forms of faith. Here we have a virtual laboratory of the power of sacramental Catholicism; in it, we can see both how the sacraments seep into ordinary life and also how the sacraments can come close to becoming cultural appendages.

Virtually every renewal movement that has swept through Latin cultures offers something *apart* from the sacramental life of the church. Liberation theology offers base communities as non-sacramental ways of organizing small communities of faith. The Cursillo movement offers the *ultreya* as a kind of cell-based organizing unit in which those who have passed through the Cursillo support each other in faith. The Charismatic renewal usually fosters prayer groups that meet in homes and cultivate the sharing of the Spirit's charisms for those who have made the "Life in the Spirit Seminars." Even Pope Paul VI extolled the possibilities of "popular religion" which developed from the folk faith of people, absorbing many cultural and pre-Christian forms of expression into accepted forms of Catholic piety—much of it non-sacramental.

To be sure, these renewal movements highlight the difficul-ties that arise from a sacramentally based evangelization—the formalism which can so identify with a culture that it becomes like any other element in that culture, losing its ability to call, challenge and shape people anew; and the dependency on sacramental ministers, with all the requisites such ministers have to fulfill before they can be authorized. That is why a sacra-mentally based evangelization, with all that it has to offer, needs to be steeped in self-criticism or else it will lose its vitality and even its accessibility.

In their fullest understanding and practice, however, the sacraments need nothing *else;* to receive them, to live them, is to be evangelized.

Sacrament and Renewal

Once the sacramental basis of evangelization is understood and accepted, however, then the place of renewal movements becomes clear. Rather than pulling away from what happens in parish and church, these movements can be seen as powerful allies of what happens in the sacramental lives of Catholics. Church can cease looking like something that gets in the way of evangelization, and personal evangelization can find the depth and support it needs in the life of the church.

All renewal movements are pointing to the same thing the sacraments are pointing to: the Christian's involvement in the paschal mystery. Although they may express themselves in language and forms which reflect some of the issues that we looked at in chapter 10, they do not have to do so. Personal faith in Jesus and the immediate action of the Holy Spirit can make church look mostly like a convenience or even an afterthought. Likewise, small groups in which Christians intensely support each other can make the parish community look bland and blah, just as they can make the life of the ordinary Catholic look mechanical and routine, if not hypocritical. But such judgments overlook what actually happens through the process of worship and often what is actually happening in the lives of believers. All believers must face the issue of constantly dying and rising in Christ Jesus. Indeed, when we looked at the mass in chapter 7, we were able, through the prism of evangelization, to see it as something like the ultimate "altar call," the ultimate call to conversion and renewal. The sacraments, with their personal and cultural weight, are not alien to renewal.

Perhaps two simple criteria can help express the alliance that sacramental and renewal forms of evangelization should have:

Is the life of the parish making it possible for people to experience renewal in one form or another?

In other words, acknowledging a "catholicity" in the ways that people are evangelized and continue to be evangelized, does the experience of worship lead people to face this ongoing conversion in their lives? Not all will be attracted to small discussion groups; only a percentage of mainline believers will be able to express themselves through the spirituality of Charismatic renewal, or any other renewal movement. But granting that every Catholic has to become ever more deeply implicated in the dying and rising of Jesus in his or her personal life, do they feel drawn and supported, by their sacramental life, to become involved in the way of renewal the Holy Spirit may be leading them to? Or does a somewhat rote-like practice of faith actually keep people away from renewal?

Do renewal movements draw people to deeper sacramental lives and to support the local parish?

Does the renewal movement draw energy from the local parish, or foster a kind of inward-looking self-absorption that forms a smaller and smaller circle as it grows in intensity? Or a kind of elitist group that sits in judgment upon everyone else? So often renewal movements end up with pockets of those who have passed through one or another special experience whose members primarily talk to themselves and who look upon others only as potential candidates for a particular retreat or seminar or renewal experience.

We are, after all, calling people to the church, to parish, to the sacraments, for all that the sacraments can be and bring about in their lives. Renewal movements can be ways to involve people more fully in parish life as it leads people to greater understanding of what it means to follow Christ, to die and rise daily, and to experience this in the receiving of Christ's sacred sacraments. Perhaps a test for their integration in the parish is the level of judgment they feel they must pass on the "ordinary Catholic" who "just comes to church." Of course the ordinary

Catholic must be called to deeper holiness; but so does everyone else!

Dealing with the Mystery

When, at the age of seven, I was being prepared for first holy communion, I remember returning to my pew after we had gone up to the altar rail and been taught how to extend our tongues. I was looking around at my fellow potential first communicants to see what they were making of the experience. From out of nowhere, Sister appeared—not our regular teacher, but the Sister who was chosen to organize the first communion celebration.

"Young man," she said with a hint of hardness, "bury your hands in your face because you have just received God!"

The gesture, burying my hand in my face, became a way for me to begin to deal with what "receiving God" meant. It stayed with me for a while (perhaps encouraged by Sister's not so gentle gaze), and then went on to become the recitation of certain prayers and, for the last three decades of my life, moments of quiet. Yet I will never grasp what it means to "receive God," or the mystery of God's drawing so close in my own life, let alone in the life of the church. What the gesture did, however, was what the sacrament ultimately does: made me deal with that mystery and its still-unfolding implications in my life.

That's what the sacraments do, make us deal with mystery, and as such they constitute the most powerful evangelizing force that God has placed at our disposal.

Appendix:
A Summary of
Go and Make Disciples:
A National Plan and Strategy for
Catholic Evangelization in the
*United States**

"Go, therefore, and make disciples of all nations, baptizing them in the name of the Father, and of the Son, and of the Holy Spirit, teaching them to observe all that I have commanded you. And behold, I am with you always, until the end of the age." Matthew 28:19–20

"I have come to set the earth on fire, and how I wish it were already blazing." Luke 12:49

Go and Make Disciples: A National Plan and Strategy for Catholic Evangelization in the United States begins by presenting gospel stories in which Jesus healed the blind Bartimaeus (Mark 10:46-52), cured the centurion's servant (Luke 7:1-10), spoke to the Samaritan woman at the well (John 4:7-42) and raised Lazarus from the dead (John 11:1-45). Each of these people, touched by

---

* The actual wording of the U.S. bishops is contained in the bold text. The reader is encouraged to read the whole plan which can be ordered from the USCC by calling 1-800-235-USCC, publication number 556-9. The entire text, along with a commentary and planning guide prepared by the present author and Fr. Kenneth Boyack, CSP, can be ordered from the Paulist National Catholic Evangelization Association by calling 1-800-237-5515.

Christ Jesus, responded to him and became part of the gospel story, the history of salvation. The bishops affirm:

> **We have become, through the power and truth of these stories, and through the free gift of grace, disciples of Jesus.**
> **We have heard [these Gospel stories], and they will not let us rest. They burn and they still set us ablaze!**

PART I
A VISION OF CATHOLIC EVANGELIZATION

Introduction

The bishops of the United States, as followers of Jesus and pastors, address all Catholics as believers, asking them to acknowledge their own experience of faith as Catholics.

> **We say it about ourselves as bishops: God has touched our lives in Jesus, bestowed his Spirit, given us salvation and hope, and called us to live in witness to his love.**
> **We know this is true of you as well: you have received the Spirit of Christ Jesus which brings salvation and hope; your lives are a witness of faith. Whether you were baptized as a child, or joined the Church as an adult, you have a story of faith. Whether you sincerely live your faith in quiet or have a great public ministry, you have a story of faith. Whether you have a grade school knowledge of the catechism or have a theological degree, you have a story of faith.**

What Is Evangelization?

The bishops define evangelization and spell out its implication for us.

> **[E]vangelizing means bringing the Good News of Jesus into every human situation and seeking to convert individu-**

als and society by the divine power of the Gospel itself. (*On Evangelization in the Modern World*, 18.) Its essence is the proclamation of salvation in Jesus Christ and the response of a person in faith, both being the work of the Spirit of God. Evangelization must always be directly connected to the Lord Jesus Christ. "There is no true evangelization if the name, the teaching, the promises, the Kingdom and the mystery of Jesus of Nazareth, the Son of God are not proclaimed" (*On Evangelization in the Modern World*, 22).

Because evangelization is about conversion, the bishops talk about the change that occurs in believers through the power of the gospel and the Holy Spirit. They point out that conversion happens in many ways—through sudden changes and through gradual growth, in children as well as adults—but that each of us must experience this fundamental change.

Conversion is the change of our lives which comes about through the power of the Holy Spirit. This is crucial: we must be converted—and we must continue to be converted! We must let the Holy Spirit change our lives! We must respond to Jesus Christ. And we must be open to the transforming power of the Holy Spirit who will continue to convert us as we follow Christ. If our faith is alive, it will be aroused again and again as we mature as disciples.

Evangelization brings about change in both individuals and society. While each of us must undergo personal renewal, the gospel also addresses society itself. Conversion is both personal and social.

The fruit of evangelization is changed lives and a changed world—holiness and justice, spirituality and peace. The validity of our having accepted the Gospel does not only come from what we feel or what we know; it comes also from the way we serve others, especially the poorest, the most marginal, the most hurting, the most defenseless, the

least loved. An evangelization that stays inside ourselves is not an evangelization into the Good News of Jesus Christ.

Evangelization happens through the power of the proclamation of the gospel. Trickery, manipulation and proselytism (using undue pressure) have no place in the proclamation of the gospel.

This vision we share is the power of the Good News. As it compels us, we believe it can compel, by its beauty and truth, all who sincerely seek God. How different our world would be if everyone could accept the Good News of Jesus and share the vision of faith!

The result of evangelization is discipleship: when people are following the Lord with hearts converted, united in community with other believers, sharing in the sacraments and serving others by bringing the good news.

We want to make it clear that evangelization means something special for us as Catholics. We can see what it means by looking at what happens to evangelized people. Not only are they related to Jesus by accepting his Gospel and receiving his Spirit; even more, their lives are changed by becoming disciples, that is, participants in the Church, celebrating God's love in worship and serving others as Jesus did (*On Evangelization in the Modern World,* 24).

Some might think of evangelization solely in terms of Jesus and our relationship with him. Yet our relationship with Jesus is found in our relationship with the community of Jesus—the Church. The way to Christ is through the community in which he lives.

Why We Evangelize

The bishops state:

We must evangelize because the Lord Jesus commanded us to. He gave the Church the unending task of evangelizing as a restless power, to stir and to stimulate all its actions until all nations have heard his Good News and until every person has become his disciple.

The bishops point out the many motives we have for evangelizing: people's hunger for the Good News, their resistance to it, their need for enlightenment and for spiritual communion, and the beauty of the gospel message itself. Then they state:

Finally, the Lord gave us yet another reason to evangelize: our love for every person, whatever his or her situation, language, physical, mental or social condition. Because we have experienced the love of Christ, we want to share it. The gifts God has given to us are not gifts for ourselves.

How Evangelization Happens

The bishops teach that evangelization happens through the power of the Holy Spirit; in fact, they say that "without the Holy Spirit, evangelization simply cannot occur." It takes place both by the way we live our faith and by the way we share our faith with others. By living our faith—in church, home and work, and with family, friends and neighbors—we bear witness to it.

The Spirit brings about evangelization in the life of the Church and in the Church's sharing the Gospel with others. Through the ordinary patterns of our Catholic life, the Holy Spirit brings about conversion and a new life in Christ.

Here there are two elements at work: *witness*, which is the simple living of the faith; and *sharing*, which is spreading the Good News of Jesus in an explicit way.

Beyond living our faith in witness, we have to share our faith with others, particularly those who have stopped practicing their Catholic faith and those who belong to no church or who belong

only nominally. In addition, we also share our faith with those
from other church communities, welcoming those who wish to
join us in the fullness of the Catholic faith.

> **Certainly, our families, parishes, associations, schools,
> hospitals, charitable works and institutions give powerful
> witness to the faith. But do they share it? Does their living
> faith lead to the conversion of minds and hearts to Jesus
> Christ? Does the fire of the Holy Spirit blaze in them? This
> plan and strategy wants to make Catholics in the United
> States, individually and as a Church, better sharers of God's
> Good News.**

The bishops also speak about those who have stopped practicing
their faith:

> **We want to let our inactive brothers and sisters know that
> they always have a place in the Church and that we are hurt
> by their absence—as they are. We want to show our regret
> for any misunderstandings or mistreatment. And we want to
> help them see that, however they feel about the Church, we
> want to talk with them, share with them, and accept them as
> brothers and sisters. Every Catholic can be a minister of wel-
> come, reconciliation and understanding to those who have
> stopped practicing the faith.**

They also ask us to share our faith with those who do not belong
to a church.

> **Our plan also asks Catholics to reach out to those who do
> not belong to a faith community and to invite them to con-
> sider the power of the Gospel of Jesus which the riches of
> the Catholic Church can bring into their lives. Perhaps this
> may seem the most difficult of all the tasks evangelization
> asks of us.**

We are to share the gospel with ecumenical sensitivity, acknowledging that the Holy Spirit has begun to draw the different Christian communities together (despite grave differences that still remain) and that interreligious dialogue forms a way for Catholics to come to understand those of other faiths, particularly the Jewish people with whom God has established the covenant, and the people of Islam.

Why We Are Issuing the Plan Now

The bishops point to great religious developments in our century, culminating in the Second Vatican Council, as well as the growing reflection of the church on evangelization in the past twenty years, beginning with Pope Paul VI and continuing with Pope John Paul II. In addition, they recall their own past statements on evangelization, particularly those issued after extensive consultation with Hispanic and African American Catholics, and the recent five-hundredth anniversary of the arrival of Christianity to our shores.

All this movement and all these documents call us to reexamine our hearts and recommit our wills to the pursuit of evangelization; they motivate us to issue this plan to make evangelization a natural and normal part of Catholic life and to give evangelizers the tools and support they need to carry out this mission today.

Led in the Spirit

The bishops remind us that we have been baptized into Christ Jesus and, therefore, baptized into his ministry. We are to awaken our own baptismal grace and become evangelizers.

Jesus was led by the Spirit of God to a life of preaching and service, to the giving of himself in sacrifice. Jesus Christ sends that same Spirit upon everyone who is baptized in his name. For we have all gone down into the water of Christ and have all been anointed to bring Good News and be true disciples. (Cf. Romans

6:3-4.) We have all received his Spirit. This is not a Spirit of timidity or fear, but a bold Spirit of life, truth, joy and grace.

PART II
GOALS AND STRATEGIES

The bishops begin this second part of *Go and Make Disciples* by recalling the Pentecost scene, as the Holy Spirit descends upon the church at its beginning, with a focus on Mary and Peter as special models for our evangelizing discipleship.

> *Two people, Mary and Peter, encircled by the other disciples, receive in the tongues of flame at Pentecost a confirmation of their discipleship, of their involvement in the story of Jesus, of their role in spreading God's Good News (Acts 2:1-14).*
>
> *This is the fire of the Holy Spirit from whom all evangelization springs. May the Spirit that came upon Mary and filled the apostles also come upon us as we present the apostolic parts of our plan.*

How To Use the Plan and Strategy

The bishops say that their message should lead us to action. As individuals, groups and parishes read the plan, they should be moved to undertake evangelizing actions.

> **We envision groups of Catholics reading this plan together, discussing its implications and being stimulated by the range of suggested strategies.**

The Context of the Goals

The bishops elaborate the three goals which form the foundation of their plan and strategy for evangelization. These goals, each of which has a different focus, all go together, because we cannot evangelize effectively as Catholics without the fullness of the gospel vision. Before elaborating on these goals, however, the bishops spell out factors that form the context of the goals:

- the goals are addressed to every Catholic;
- the goals cannot be accomplished without fervent prayer;
- the plan is part of the evangelizing ministry of the whole church, in union with the Holy Father;
- the goals must bear upon our everyday life;
- the parish is central to accomplishing these goals;
- evangelization is a collaborative effort between clergy and lay people;
- the evangelizing spirit should be consistent at all levels of the church's organization;
- we will evangelize in a culture that will resist our message and make the goals difficult to accomplish.

The bishops then present the three goals and outline the strategy involved in each goal.

Goal I

TO BRING ABOUT IN ALL CATHOLICS SUCH AN ENTHUSIASM FOR THEIR FAITH THAT, IN LIVING THEIR FAITH IN JESUS, THEY FREELY SHARE IT WITH OTHERS.

The strategy of this goal is to so deepen the sense of Scripture and sacrament that Catholics will pray more fully, and, with a greater understanding of Christ's call, live as disciples at home, at work and in today's many cultural settings. This goal also seeks a greater openness to physical, mental and cultural diversity among Catholics.

This goal includes the following objectives:
- to foster an experience of conversion and renewal in each individual and every parish;
- to foster a greater appreciation of God's word in our lives;

- to highlight the evangelizing dimension of the Sunday eucharist, the power of God's word in worship, and our recognition of Christ's presence in the sacraments;
- to develop a deeper life of prayer among Catholics;
- to instill a renewed understanding of the faith among Catholics;
- to foster a sense of being disciples among Catholic adults and children;
- to create small group experiences of prayer and study;
- to foster a greater sense of our homes as domestic churches;
- to develop a spirituality for the workplace;
- to foster greater appreciation of cultural and spiritual diversity.

Goal II

TO INVITE ALL PEOPLE IN THE UNITED STATES, WHATEVER THEIR SOCIAL OR CULTURAL BACK-GROUND, TO HEAR THE MESSAGE OF SALVATION IN JESUS CHRIST SO THEY MAY COME TO JOIN US IN THE FULLNESS OF THE CATHOLIC FAITH.

The strategy behind this goal is to create a more welcoming attitude toward others in our parishes so that people feel at home; next, to create an attitude of sharing faith and to develop greater skills to do this; then to undertake activities to invite others to know the Catholic people better.

This second goal, which concentrates on the outward dimension of evangelization, includes these objectives:
- to make every Catholic institution more welcoming;
- to help every Catholic feel comfortable about sharing his or her faith;
- to develop within families and households the capacity to share the gospel;
- to train Catholics to be evangelizers;

- to use special family and parish times to invite people to faith;
- to form a core of people to serve as ministers of evangelization in a special way;
- to effectively invite people to our church, both on a parish and on a national level;
- to design programs that reach out in particular ways to those who have no church and those who seek the fullness of faith;
- to effectively welcome back those who have left the church;
- to foster an appreciation of cultural diversity;
- to deepen ecumenical involvement in the church.

Goal III

TO FOSTER GOSPEL VALUES IN OUR SOCIETY, PROMOTING THE DIGNITY OF THE HUMAN PERSON, THE IMPORTANCE OF THE FAMILY, AND THE COMMON GOOD OF OUR SOCIETY, SO THAT OUR NATION MAY CONTINUE TO BE TRANSFORMED BY THE SAVING POWER OF JESUS CHRIST.

This goal means supporting those cultural elements in our land that reflect Catholic values and challenging those which reject it. Catholics, who today are involved in every level of modern life in the United States, have to address our society as a system and also in particular situations.

This goal requires the strategy of strengthening our everyday involvement with those in need, of reflecting on the workplace and media, and of encouraging Catholic involvement in areas of public policy as a way of having greater impact on society's values.

This goal calls us to pursue these objectives:
- to involve parishes and local service groups in alleviating the immediate needs of people in their areas;
- to foster the importance of the family;

- to explore issues of our workplaces and lay spirituality;
- to encourage Catholic witness in the arts and intellectual community;
- to involve Catholics on every level in areas of public policy, in the media and in questions of economic systems.

Invitation and Implementation

The bishops, taking the responsibility and initiative for the plan in their own dioceses, invite us to make this plan our own by acknowledging our ability to bring good news to others in our personal lives, through our family life and through our parishes. They pledge their support and ask our support in turn. They ask the help of Catholics as individuals, as families, and as members of parishes to put the plan into action. In addition, they appeal to Catholic institutions like schools and hospitals, as well as Catholic organizations, to use this plan as a basis for reflection and action.

We offer the Catholics of the United States the same invitation as Jesus: Come and follow! Come, hear the Lord calling each one of us; come, follow the Teacher who makes us his disciples. Come, be part of the story of salvation.

Our invitation asks every believer to discover ways that he or she can realize this plan in every way appropriate— personally, in the family, in the neighborhood and parish, or as part of a larger organization.

We invite you: Make this plan *your* plan.

A Concluding Prayer

As we present this plan to our brother and sister Catholics in the United States, we pray that, through the Holy Spirit, it may be a means of bringing renewal to our church and new life to all who search for God.

We pray that the fire of Jesus enkindled in us by God's Spirit may lead more and more people in our land to become disciples, formed in the image of Christ our Savior.